Preface for the Confirmed Catholic

When you are confirmed, you receive the Holy Spirit's fullest measure of Divine Graces, which are now at your disposal—*but not without effort!* The Holy Spirit guides you to the extent you are an active participant in doing the Will of God. But this may not be easy. The world no longer follows the teachings of the Catholic Church.

In many quarters, the teachings of the Church are now questioned as old-fashioned or irrational. Many people now prefer to "believe in science," but science does not require belief—science deals with analysis of theories about material realities that can be proven. What people really mean to say is that they no longer believe in non-material realities. But, as Shakespeare's Hamlet reminds his friend Horatio: *"There are more things in Heaven and earth than are dreamt of in your philosophy."*

Saint Paul tell us that everything in our Faith depends on Jesus Christ. If He is not the Son of God who died on the Cross and rose from the dead to save us from sin and death and open the gates of Heaven, then "our faith is in vain." Jesus is who He said He was; if not, He was a madman. And if Jesus truly is the Son of God who came among us as a man "like us in all things except sin," then everything He said is true: "I Am the Way, the Truth, and the Life."

There is no way to PROVE that Jesus is God; it is a matter of faith. You have been given that gift and then be *confirmed* in that gift of faith. But Confirmation is not the end of your growth as a Christian—it is really just the beginning.

Every generation of mankind after Jesus rose from the dead has been called upon to pass on the Faith given to them by the Apostles, who received it from Jesus. The Catholic Church has protected the treasure of the Faith by preserving the Holy Bible and the Traditions handed down from the Apostles. The Church succeeds in this effort because it is guided by the Holy Spirit, the Third Person of the Blessed Trinity, who keeps the Church's teachings on faith and morals free from error. We are each an instrument of God's graces if we remain faithful to what the Church teaches. Every generation must protect and defend the Faith by living it and passing it on. ***Now it is your turn to live it and to pass it on***.

Know that God loves you and that He always hears you when you pray. He may not answer you in the way you expect, but He walks with you through all the joys and sufferings of life. He does not ask you to go where He has not been—if you die to yourself in Christ, you will surely live with Him forever in Heaven.

The graces of Confirmation are your sword and shield in the battle of good over evil in this world. Now you are truly prepared to become ***Heroes of Grace***!

The Book of Sevens of the Catholic Faith
Table of Contents

The Seven Sacraments

The Sacraments are **outward signs instituted by Christ to give grace**. Jesus understood that we are physical, as well as spiritual, beings. The sensible sign of each Sacrament helps us to grasp the unseen spiritual gift that is given when we receive one of the seven Sacraments. Each Sacrament has a specific outward sign that is associated with a distinct Divine gift of sanctifying grace. Grace is the Divine Life of God that He gives us to help us in our life journey home to Heaven. The graces we receive are the result of Jesus Christ's saving act—as the altarpiece pictured here demonstrates, by showing that all the graces of the Sacraments flow from the Cross.

Christ's Perfect Sacrifice atoned for all the sins of mankind. In this way, Jesus opened the gates of Heaven and allowed the gifts of grace that God desires to give us in the Holy Spirit to flow out through the Sacraments.

The Seven Sacraments Altarpiece, by Rogier van der Weyden, c1450. Royal Museum of Fine Arts, Antwerp. Public Domain.

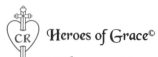
The Sacrament of Baptism

Baptism Window, St. Mary's, Tennessee. Released to Public Domain by Gary Bridgman.

Public Domain.

dead to the life of Divine grace is cleansed of all sin and made a member of the Body of Christ and a child of God. The earliest Christians knew this well—they spoke of going into the waters of Baptism [*by immersion*] as "dying" and of coming out of the waters as "rising to new life in Christ."

In many Christian faiths, it is thought that Baptism should be reserved for consenting adults rather than for infants. However, the Catholic Church has practiced infant baptism for many hundreds of years, with the understanding that it is far more important to bring each newly created soul into the life of grace as soon as possible, so each little child can become an heir to Heaven and grow up in the embrace of God's Divine life.

One of the most important responsibilities of Catholic parents is to have their child baptized as soon as possible. In the event of an emergency, anyone can baptize another person by pouring water over them and saying the exact words Jesus spoke. Not only does this open up the life of grace for the child, it ensures their path to Heaven.

Jesus' last words to the Apostles before He ascended into Heaven were a clear command to go out and teach everyone about what He had revealed—**and to baptize them**. Baptism is the Sacrament of first Initiation into the Divine life of God. Through Baptism, we become the sons and daughters of God, a part of His family, and are made heirs to Heaven.

The Bible tells us that when Adam and Eve chose to disobey the Will of God, they separated themselves—and all their descendants—from union with God and from His graces. Their "original sin" placed a terrible barrier between the human race and God. The knowledge of evil that Adam and Eve gained by their sin brought suffering and death into human existence. The Sacrament of Baptism undoes this inherited flaw by washing away the mark of original sin from the soul of the person being baptized.

It is not possible to see the saving effects of the Sacrament of Baptism; however, the specific sign of the Sacrament of Baptism is the water that is poured over the person as the words that Jesus commanded are said. In this way, we see and hear the moment in which the soul that was

"Go forth and teach all nations, baptizing them in the Name of the Father, and of the Son, and of the Holy Spirit."

The Sacrament of Baptism. ©Nheyob, 2016. CC BY-SA 4.0.

The Sacrament of Penance

Public Domain.

When a person receives the Sacrament of Baptism, the stain of original sin is wiped away, and all sins the person actually committed by disobeying God's laws. But what about the actual sins a person commits *after* Baptism? In His wonderful mercy, God gave us the Sacrament of Penance, also called "Confession," to wipe away our actual sins and restore our souls to union with God's graces in this life.

After Jesus rose from the dead on Easter Sunday, He entered the Upper Room where the Apostles were praying together. He breathed on them and said, "Receive the Holy Spirit. If you forgive the sins of any, they are forgiven them; if you retain the sins of any, they are retained" (*John 20: 23*). At that moment, Jesus gave the Apostles (and all ordained priests who come after them) the power to forgive sins. This means that if you: 1. Examine your conscience (which should be informed by a clear knowledge of God's laws); 2 & 3. Go to Confession with sincere contrition [*sorrow for sinning*] and tell the priest your sins; 4. Promise to amend your life ["From now on do not sin again" (*John 8: 11*)]; and 5. Perform the penance the priest gives you in Confession—to show that you sincerely want to make up for the

Five Things Necessary for a Good Confession

1. Before going to Confession, examine your conscience.
2. Have contrition [*sorrow*] for your sins.
3. Make a firm resolution to never sin again.
4. Confess your sins to the priest.
5. Accept the penance the priest gives you.

harms that you caused by sinning. Though you speak to a priest, you are really speaking to God through him; then God speaks through him to give you His forgiveness. When the priest says the words of Absolution, he makes the Sign of the Cross—the outward sign that you have received a great spiritual gift: *you are reconciled to God!*

When examining your conscience, consider the sins that are serious [*mortal*], as well as sins that are not as serious [*venial*]. Mortal sins should be confessed as soon as possible because they cut us off entirely from God's Divine Life. It is a good spiritual practice to go to Confession once a month in order to receive all the graces God desires to give you to help you to resist temptation and rise above your failings. To those who say one should go directly to God to confess, remember what Jesus said to the ten lepers who asked to be healed: "Go and show yourselves to the priests."

Konfeso [Confession], by Phillipp Schumacher, in Katholisches Religionsbuchlein, ed. Wilhelm Pichler, 1920. Public Domain.

THE WORDS OF ABSOLUTION

"God, the Father of mercies, through the death and resurrection of His Son, has reconciled the world to Himself and sent the Holy Spirit among us for the forgiveness of sins. Through the ministry of the Church, may God give you pardon and peace, and I absolve you from your sins in the Name of the Father and of the Son, and of the Holy Spirit. Amen."

THE BOOK OF SEVENS

The Sacrament of the Body and Blood of Christ

Public Domain.

The Last Supper: The First Holy Mass.
©*Reinhardhauke, 2010. CC BY-SA 3.0.*

but He did even more—He offered His "Flesh" as "true Food" (*John 6: 55*). Jesus found a way to unite Himself with every person in every generation to come—so He could remain with us "until the end of the age" (*Matt. 28: 20*). From earliest Christian times, the Holy Eucharist has been reverenced as the actual Body and Blood of Christ, "confected" by the miracle of transubstantiation, in which the sensible properties of bread and wine remain the same, but the Essence is changed into the Real Presence of Our Lord. When Jesus explained this to the Jews in *John 6*, many walked away in disbelief. However, Jesus did not call them back—He did not say His words were just symbolic. Instead, He spoke even more graphically:

> "*Very truly, I tell you, unless you eat the Flesh of the Son of Man and drink His Blood, you have no life in you. Those who eat My Flesh and drink My Blood have eternal life, and I will raise them up on the last day; for My Flesh is true Food and My Blood is true Drink. Those who eat My Flesh and drink My Blood abide in Me, and I in them. ... the one who eats this Bread will live forever.*" (53-55, 58)

Among many titles—Blessed Sacrament, Sacrament of the Altar, Real Presence—the title **Holy Eucharist** focuses on the Holy Sacrifice of the Mass. "Eucharist" in Greek means "*giving thanks.*" Just so, the Mass is the celebration of our relationship with God: we offer ourselves to God with love and thanks, and He gives us His Son in return, thereby uniting us with God in a "spiritual wedding feast." Why would anyone *not* choose to fulfill their weekly obligation to love and be loved by God and to sanctify the world by attending Mass? **What is more important?**

The night before Jesus died on the Cross, He shared the Passover Seder meal with His Apostles. The Seder commemorates the night during the Jews' captivity as slaves in Egypt when the Angel of Death "passed over" all the houses where the blood of a sacrificial lamb had been painted on the door posts, thus sparing the lives of the Jews within.

This Seder is called the "Last Supper" because it was Jesus' last meal before He died, but it was also the *first Mass*. Jesus offered Himself as the Lamb of God to be slain for our sins so that we could be saved from the slavery of sin and death. During the meal, He offered bread and wine, saying, "this is My Body" and "this is My Blood of the covenant, which is poured out for many for the forgiveness of sins" (*Matt. 26: 28*). He offered Himself as the sacrificial Lamb,

Through Him, and with Him, and in Him, O God Almighty Father, in the unity of the Holy Spirit, all Glory and Honor is Yours, for ever and ever. AMEN.

Omnis Honor et Gloria ["All Honor and Glory"]. ©Andreas F. Borchert, 2012. CC BY-SA 3.0.

The Sacrament of Confirmation

"I sign you with the Sign of the Cross, and I confirm you with the chrism of salvation, in the Name of the Father, and of the Son, and of the Holy Spirit."

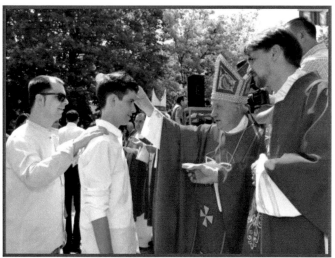

Candidate Receives the Sacrament of Confirmation, May 19, 2013. Released to Public Domain by Zvonimir Corie. Catholic News Agency, Bishops' Conference of Bosnia Herzegovina.

Like the Sacrament of Baptism, Confirmation can only be received once in a person's lifetime. Like Baptism, Confirmation puts an indelible mark on the soul of the person receiving the graces of this Sacrament. The graces received at Baptism are *confirmed* and strengthened by the Sacrament of Confirmation; the person's soul is now given a full measure of the Seven Gifts of the Holy Spirit. As the Apostles first received the anointing of the Holy Spirit in "tongues as of fire" on Pentecost Sunday, each of the newly confirmed is given the powers needed to stand firm in the Faith. The newly confirmed receive the strength to defend the Faith, to share it with a world that does not always understand it, and to remain faithful witnesses to the truth of Jesus Christ and His teachings—what has been called since the early years of the Church "becoming a soldier of Christ."

The Bishop is the ordinary minister of the

The Seven Gifts of the Holy Spirit as Tongues of Fire.
©Reinhardhauke, 2011. CC BY-SA 3.0.

Sacrament of Confirmation, although priests are allowed to confirm in special circumstances—if they have first received permission from their bishop. This is often the case for those converts being received into the Church at Easter Vigil; they receive both the Sacraments of Baptism and Confirmation at the same time, administered by the priest saying the Easter Vigil Mass.

As part of the Rite of Confirmation, the bishop or priest uses holy chrism to make the Sign of the Cross on the candidate's head while he speaks the words of the Sacrament (*shown above*). After this, he makes a gesture as he offers each candidate the Peace of Christ. In years past, the bishop would tap the candidate's cheek in a symbolic "slap" to suggest the challenges that the candidate may have to face in defense of the Faith. After the Second Vatican Council, this gesture, while still allowed as part of the Rite, may also be expressed as a handshake or other friendly gesture.

The Seven Gifts of the Holy Spirit are these:
- **Wisdom**: the love of spiritual things
- **Understanding**: the power to grasp the Faith
- **Counsel**: the ability to discern right from wrong
- **Fortitude**: the strength to risk all for Christ
- **Knowledge**: the power to know the things of God
- **Piety**: the duty to worship God with reverence
- **Fear of the Lord**: the wonder and awe needed to appreciate and give glory to the majesty of God.

The Sacrament of Matrimony

Public Domain.

Public Domain.

The Wedding Feast at Cana [Detail]. ©Nheyob, 2013. CC BY-SA 3.0.

> " I, (...), take you, (...),
> to be my lawfully wedded
> (husband/wife),
> to have and to hold,
> from this day forward,
> for better, for worse,
> for richer, for poorer,
> in sickness and in health,
> until death do us part."

The Catholic Church has always taught that marriage is a sacred covenant between a man and a woman—a lifelong, exclusive commitment to loving, serving, and supporting each other till "death do us part," and to raising any children with which God blesses them in a loving, secure home. This commitment is made during the Sacrament of Matrimony. A priest witnesses the vows of the couple, but the "minister" of this Sacrament is the man and the woman who make promises of lifelong fidelity to each other; their vows are the outward sign of the Sacrament.

Vows spoken in the Sacrament of Matrimony bind the couple to each other for life. Their love is far more than physical attraction or pleasure. Their love mirrors the love of the Holy Trinity; the union of their lives in body and soul reflects the union of the Holy Trinity—a love so fruitful between God the Father and God the Son that the result is a Third Person—God the Holy Spirit. God dignifies marital love to the degree that their love, when open to the possibility of life, may participate in the creation of another human being—an immense power that in God's plan is designed to be shared with married couples. In this way, their relationship is life-giving and fruitful, blessing the love they share with more love—sometimes in the form of a child.

Unlike a relationship in which two lovers seek personal gratification from each other, true sacramental marriage happens when a man and woman promise to love each other exclusively all their lives, sharing the good and bad together and remaining open to the creation of new life. Marriage is not a "50/50" proposition—it is 100/100; it requires giving one's whole self to the beloved without reservation, no matter what the future may hold. When a man and woman make their love holy through the Sacrament of Matrimony, Jesus abides with them and gives them all the graces they need to love each other faithfully.

The Sacrament of Holy Orders

Only a bishop can perform the Sacrament of Holy Orders. Every ordained bishop can trace his Holy Orders to one of the Apostles, who received their spiritual powers from Jesus. The powers of the priesthood have been handed down through the centuries directly from Jesus.

Like Baptism and Confirmation, the Sacrament of Holy Orders can only be conferred once. The soul of the man receiving Holy Orders is changed forever, given a spiritual character which makes it possible for him to offer the Holy Sacrifice

Public Domain.

of the Mass, confect the Blessed Sacrament, and perform other duties, such as serving as God's intermediary by absolving sins in the Sacrament of Penance, dispensing graces through blessings, discerning spirits, and offering daily prayers for the Church.

When a man is ordained a priest during the Sacrament of Holy Orders, he becomes an *alter Christus* [another Christ]. When an ordained priest speaks the words of Consecration: "*This is My Body*" and "*This is the Chalice of My Blood*," his soul is united to Jesus in such a way that Jesus acts *through him* to become Present in the bread and wine, which are changed into Jesus's Body and Blood by a transformative miracle called **Transubstantiation**. The bread and wine change—but not in their appearance. The *substance* of the bread and wine is altered; the Sacred Elements *become* the living Presence of Jesus, who promised to remain with us until the end of time.

As part of the ceremony of the Sacrament of Holy Orders, the priests' hands are anointed with holy oils, as seen in both illustrations on this page. The priest's fingers that touch the Sacred Elements—the first finger and thumb— are held in particular respect. For hundreds of years before the Second Vatican Council in 1965, only priests were permitted to touch the Sacred Elements. It is a great privilege (and an exception to the Norm of receiving on the tongue)

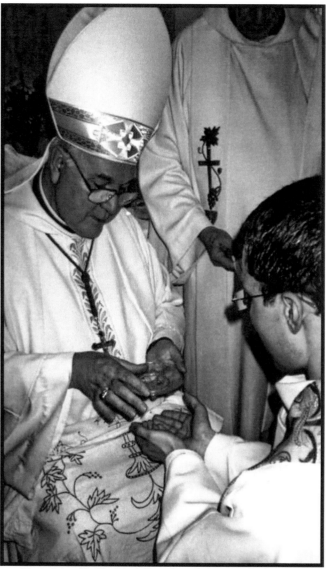

The Anointing of the New Priest's Fingers during the Sacrament of Holy Orders. Montreal, August 15, 2007. ©English nol,2007. CC BY-SA 3.0.

that lay people in some countries are allowed the choice to receive Holy Communion in the hand.

The role of an ordained priest is to mediate between God and man. When he offers the Holy Sacrifice of the Mass, he mediates between God and the people in the church, who unite with him in offering God all their prayers, works, joys, and sufferings. By the power of his priesthood, these offerings are united to the Perfect Sacrifice that Jesus offered in His death on the Cross. In this way, the people participate in the fruits of that Perfect Sacrifice, receiving graces to help restore the world to goodness and give Glory to God.

The Sacrament of the Sick

Public Domain.

The Sacrament of the Sick, which was once known as Extreme Unction, is available to all Catholics who have reached the age of reason and are experiencing serious suffering in body or soul. The minister of this Sacrament is the priest, who prays over the sick person and uses holy oils to anoint the person's hands and feet. Once feared as a sign of an imminent death, the Sacrament of the Sick is now seen as appropriate for anyone who is elderly (and in good health), or about to undergo serious surgery, or who has been involved in a serious accident.

The effects of the Sacrament are an increase in sanctifying grace, added strength and comfort to deal with the challenges of the sick person's unique sufferings, and, in some cases, the Sacrament also assists in helping to heal the person physically! Either way, the Sacrament of the Sick always prepares the person's soul for their heavenly home, should God's Will decide that it would be best for that person to go to their Heavenly inheritance rather than recover.

Whenever someone is seriously ill or reaching an advanced age, it is wise to make sure that the person receives the Sacrament of the Sick. It is always better to provide them with the graces and comfort of the Sacrament, rather than to delay

and risk the loss of these healing graces that relieve fears and temptations to despair in the midst of suffering while they prepare the soul for whatever destiny God's Will has ordained.

Even after a person dies, a brief period of time still remains when a priest can anoint the body and give conditional absolution to the person's soul.

When a person is facing the real probability that they may die, it is usual to give them the Last Rites. The priest will hear their confession, give them absolution, and offer them the comfort of receiving Holy Communion. In this case, the reception of Holy Communion is often called Viaticum. This word comes from the Latin for "provision for the journey" and refers to the fact that the dying person who receives Jesus in Holy Communion does not die alone, but in the arms of Our Lord.

The Sacrament of the Sick. [Holy Eucharist].
©Romke Hoekstra, 2007. CC BY-SA 3.0.

It has been a longstanding tradition that every Catholic home should have at least one blessed candle, a crucifix, and holy water, so that, in the event that a priest is called to the home to give the Last Rites to a dying person, the sacramentals that are required will be readily available.

The Seven Gifts of the Holy Spirit

The Pentecost Chapel at Lourdes. Released to Public Domain by Tangopaso, 2010.

The Gifts of the Holy Spirit

Wisdom

Understanding

Counsel

Knowledge

Fortitude

Piety

Fear of the Lord

The Fruits of the Holy Spirit

Charity

Joy

Peace

Patience

Kindness

Goodness

Constancy

Gentleness

Faith

Modesty

Continency

Chastity

The Gifts of the Holy Spirit are seven kinds of inspiration received in the Sacrament of Baptism and confirmed [made complete] in the Sacrament of Confirmation. Because the Holy Spirit, third Person of the Blessed Trinity, is the Love Personified between God the Father and God the Son, these gifts are a sharing in the Divine Life of God. The Gifts of the Holy Spirit are powers that come directly from God. Like the tongues of fire that came down at Pentecost upon the Apostles, the Gifts of the Holy Spirit communicate God's holy inspirations directly into our souls to help us achieve what can surpass our natural capabilities. To make full use of these gifts, we must remain in a state of grace [without any serious sins], seek to remain open to the promptings of the Holy Spirit, and to ask for these gifts.

Saint Paul, in his letter to the Galatians, names twelve fruits identified with the use of the Gifts of the Holy Spirit: Charity [Love], Joy, Peace, Patience, Benignity [Kindness], Goodness, Longanimity [Constancy/Long-Suffering], Mildness [Gentleness], Faith, Modesty, Continency [Self-Control], and Chastity. Those who makes use of the Gifts of the Holy Spirit bring benefits to every person who comes in contact with them. They sow the seeds of joy and peace in the world. They are blessed with inner peace, abiding joy, spiritual strength, and purity of heart in spite of life's struggles, disappointments, and sufferings.

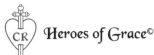

The Seven Gifts of the Holy Spirit
WISDOM

In his Old Testament book, the Prophet Isaiah describes the Gifts of the Holy Spirit in chapter 11, verses 2-3 [*quoted in sidebar at right*]. These Gifts, the direct inspirations freely given by the Holy Spirit, assist us in persevering in virtue in two ways. The first group—Wisdom, Understanding, Counsel, Knowledge—inspires our <u>mind</u> to receive the Spirit's promptings so that we may achieve a deeper appreciation of God. The second group—Fortitude, Piety, and Fear of the Lord—prompts our <u>will</u> so we may learn to accept God's Will and choose to do what it right accordingly.

The first and most perfect gift is Wisdom, defined in the dictionary as "the ability to discern what is right, to show good judgment." But the Holy Spirit's Wisdom is more: His Wisdom helps us to recognize the things of God and to love them more than the things of this world. This Wisdom helps us to see beyond the world around us so we can grasp the deeper meaning of life.

The Bible tells us that the wisest man who ever lived was King Solomon. When he was still young, he was made King of Judah. In a dream, God invited him to ask for whatever he wanted: Solomon asked for great wisdom so that he could rule his kingdom with justice and kindness. God was so pleased with this request that He told Solomon He would give him greater wisdom than any man who lived before or after him.

The wisdom of Solomon is legendary, and many stories in the Bible attest to this. Solomon himself wrote a book in the Bible called *Wisdom*, in which he describes the value and beauty of this gift of Wisdom. Solomon's own words describing Wisdom are quoted in the sidebar at right (*Wisdom* 7: 7-10, 14).

> **The Spirit of the Lord shall rest upon him,**
> **the spirit of wisdom and understanding,**
> **the spirit of counsel and might,**
> **the spirit of knowledge and the fear of the LORD.**
> **And his delight shall be in the fear of the LORD.**
>
> —*Isaiah 11: 2-3. Ignatius Revised Standard Edition.*

As Solomon shows in his book, the gift of Wisdom helps to separate us from an attachment to the things of this world, which, while they may seem desirable and beautiful within the context of the material world, are not comparable to the riches and beauty of the treasures of Heaven. The Holy Spirit's Gift of Wisdom provides us with the special vision needed to see beyond this world so we can desire the things of Heaven and love the things of God—Truth, Goodness, Beauty, Justice, and Love. Once we have this vision, we can chart a course through life that recognizes what is most important.

King Solomon from Gustave Doré's illustrations for the Book of Proverbs, 1866. Public Domain.

> *I called upon God, and the spirit of wisdom came to me.*
> *I preferred her to scepters and thrones, and I accounted wealth as nothing in comparison with her. Neither did I liken to her any priceless gem, because all gold is but a little sand in her sight. . . . I loved her more than health and beauty, and I chose to have her rather than light, . . . for those who get her treasure obtain friendship with God.*
>
> —*Wisdom 7: 7-10, 14. Ignatius Revised Standard Edition.*

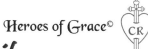

The Seven Gifts of the Holy Spirit
UNDERSTANDING

One of the ways the Holy Spirit guides our minds is through the Gift of Understanding. Human beings are endowed with many powers of thought. From the time of the ancient philosophers, a kind of reasoning called **speculative thought** has been identified as one of the ways that the human mind tries to apprehend the truth.

Speculative thought comes from that part of the mind that can examine an idea or formulate a theory using deductive reasoning and logic. *Thinking in the abstract* is another way this mental process can be described. These abilities are natural to the human mind, but when we add the promptings of the Holy Spirit to inspire the mind to understand the truths of God, then we are looking at the Gift of Understanding as the Holy Spirit freely gives it.

One of the greatest examples of a person whose speculative reason made full use of the Holy Spirit's Gift of Understanding is Saint Thomas Aquinas. Adding to the fact that he is often described by the secular culture as one of the ten greatest intellects in history, Saint Thomas Aquinas took all these powers of reasoning and applied them to the study of God—what we call *theology*. He wrote many books about theology that are still studied today as masterpieces of logic and deductive reasoning that explain more clearly than anyone else the mysteries of God and the truths of the Catholic Faith. His most famous book is called the *Summa Theologica*.

When a person makes use of the Gift of Understanding, the mind listens to the inspirations of the Holy Spirit as it strives to make sense of the truth as revealed by Jesus Christ and handed down from the Apostles through the ages by the Church's Magisterium [teaching authority]. In this way, a Christian who is open to the promptings of the Holy Spirit can understand what is right, what is wrong, and what is self-evident—based upon the truth. This Gift brings with it the assurance that the Holy Spirit will be there to guide us to know what we need to know in order to understand the truth.

Saint Thomas Aquinas by Fra Angelico. Public Domain.

The Seven Gifts of the Holy Spirit
COUNSEL

The Holy Spirit's Gift of Understanding helps the mind to figure out what God wants us to know about the truths He has revealed. The Gift of Counsel works on a more practical level. With Counsel, the Holy Spirit inspires us to make good choices with regard to our *actions*; when the Holy Spirit gives the Gift of Counsel, He aids the mind in making choices to do the good and avoid the evil in daily life.

The Gift of Counsel helps us to order our lives prudently according to God's laws, so we may always make choices that are good for our own salvation and for the Glory of God. This Gift of Counsel is sometimes called "Right Judgment" to indicate that it inspires the person who remains open to the Holy Spirit to live out the Gospel values that Jesus laid out for us when He taught us what God desires us to do.

God has provided many forms of assistance in helping us to decide which actions are good and which are bad. He has given us the Ten Commandments in the Old Testament to show us what He does not want us to do and the Eight Beatitudes in the New Testament to show us what He does want us to do. He gives us the Supernatural Virtues of Faith, Hope, and Charity at Baptism to form our souls for His Divine Life and to lead us to make choices that bring us closer to Him rather than further away. He gives us seven Sacraments so He can share more of His Divine Life—His graces—with us, especially the Sacrament of Penance to help us return to the right path when we stray and the Sacrament of Holy Eucharist to give us the strength to persevere in the right path by keeping us in union with Jesus Himself.

But there are times in life when all of these supports can still benefit from direct assistance from the Holy Spirit. Sometimes there is no way to know which choice is better or which course of action will bring us closer to God. Then the promptings of the Holy Spirit in the Gift of Counsel can make all the difference!

There is no more perfect example of a person who always did what God's Will required than the Blessed Mother. Mary never even *wanted* to do anything that was not consistent with God's Will. At the Annunciation, when Angel Gabriel came to her, she was already betrothed to Saint Joseph and planning to lead a good and holy life as his wife. But her openness to the promptings of the Holy Spirit was complete: she accepted God's unique Will for her immediately. At that moment, Mary was overshadowed by the Holy Spirit, and our Savior Jesus became Incarnate.

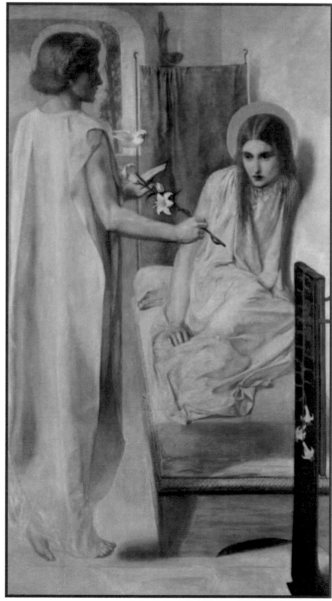

The Annunciation by Dante Gabriel Rossetti, 1849. Tate, London. Public Domain.

The Seven Gifts of the Holy Spirit
KNOWLEDGE

The dictionary defines the word *knowledge* as "the condition of knowing something through education or experience." However, the Holy Spirit's Gift of Knowledge is specific to the things of God. This Gift is not a grace to help us do well on tests or remember trivia. This kind of Knowledge concerns knowing about God and knowing God.

Philosophers have argued for centuries about whether it is possible to know God. If we reason to a conclusion, then it is impossible for us to know God—how can a finite mind know a Mind that is Infinite? How can our fallible minds comprehend the Absolute and Perfect? Yet these arguments overlook one critical aspect of this question—while it is impossible for us to reach up and know God with our minds, God can choose to look down and reveal aspects of His Being to us that we can comprehend—if we listen to the promptings of the Holy Spirit in the Gift of Knowledge. Here it is especially important to remember that the Gifts of the Holy Spirit are direct and external to our minds. We do not have to fully understand to receive these holy inspirations.

One of the best examples of a Saint who made full use of the Holy Spirit's Gift of Knowledge is Saint Catherine of Siena. Deeply in love with God from her earliest childhood, she chose to dedicate herself completely to God, refusing to get married even when her father punished her, making her the maid in her own home—with 24 brothers and sisters! Eventually convinced of her sanctity, her father gave her a room of her own—a great privilege in such a large family!

Saint Catherine never went to school; she did not know how to read or write. Yet, she had such an intimate relationship with God that she sat for hours silent and still as she communicated with Him in her soul. Sometimes she dictated her conversations with God to Blessed Raymond of Capua, collected into the book *The Dialogue*, in which she describes knowing God through His interacting with her interiorly. This type of

Saint Catherine of Siena receives the Stigmata—the Wounds of Christ.

Knowledge of God can only come *from* God, a totally gratuitous gift of the Holy Spirit. God showered Catherine with other mystical gifts, too, including the Stigmata—the same Wounds that Jesus bore on the Cross.

The Holy Spirit's Gift of the Knowledge of the things of God includes the power to teach the truths of God to others in ways that explain these truths to those who believe and defends them against those who do not believe.

The Seven Gifts of the Holy Spirit
FORTITUDE

The first four Gifts of the Holy Spirit cooperate with the _mind_ to help us know God more fully through the various ways that the human mind can encounter truth. The last three Gifts of the Holy Spirit work with the human _will_ in helping us to make choices that lead us to God.

The Gift of Fortitude, also known as Courage, fortifies our wills to remain strong regardless of whatever challenges life may present—in doing what is right and avoiding what is wrong. This strength can be the quiet determination to follow God's laws in a society that not longer recognizes them; it can be the firmness of mind needed to stand fast in the face of evil, even when the result is rejection, abuse, or even threats to physical safety. In its purest form, this Gift of the Holy Spirit is the strength to be martyred for the Faith or give one's life for another.

A Saint who gave powerful witness to this Gift in modern times by his actions is Father Maximilian Kolbe. Serving as a Conventual Franciscan friar in Poland during World War II, Father Kolbe, over time, hid 2,000 Jews in his friary from the Nazis.

Photograph of Father Maximilian Kolbe in 1939. Public Domain.

Eventually he was captured and taken to the prison camp at Auschwitz. In July 1941, three prisoners escaped from camp. The camp commander punished the rest of the prisoners by choosing at random ten men to be starved to death. When one of the ten begged to be spared because he had a wife and children, Father Kolbe stepped forward and volunteered to take his place. When the commander learned that Kolbe was a priest, he accepted the switch.

During the following two weeks that the ten men were starving to death in a dark bunker, Father Kolbe prayed and sang hymns to the Blessed Mother, whom he loved very much. He told the nine other men to rejoice—that they would soon be in Heaven with God. Finally, only Father Kolbe remained. The prison doctor gave him a lethal injection, which he calmly took; the doctor was so shamed by Father Kolbe's holiness, he asked the priest to look away. At Father Kolbe's canonization, the man whose life he had saved came with his family, wearing his Auschwitz uniform.

Father Maximilian Kolbe Window, Szombathely, Hungary. Photo Released to Public Domain.

The Seven Gifts of the Holy Spirit
PIETY

> " 'Which commandment is first of all?'
> Jesus answered, 'You shall love the Lord your God
> with all your heart, and with all your soul,
> and with all your mind, and with all your strength.'
> The second is this,
> 'You shall love your neighbor as yourself.' "
>
> (Mark 12: 30)

The Gifts of the Holy Spirit work together to help the soul attain the perfection Jesus spoke of when He said, "Be perfect, as your Heavenly Father is perfect" (Matthew 5: 48). This is never more true than with the Gift of Piety. Piety is the expression of devotion to God, and, through the knowledge of God, devotion to others and to the self.

Piety is expressed in our relationship to God. Just as children love their father and mother because their parents gave them life and care for them, all of God's children should love Him as Creator, Savior, and Sanctifier. When we recognize Who God is and who we are, our devotion to God finds expression in acts of adoration and thanksgiving. Piety is giving God all that He deserves because He is All-Powerful, All-Good, All-Beautiful, and All-Loving.

God has told us how He desires us to worship Him—not with merely external offerings, but with the offering of our hearts. He has told us *how* He desires us to offer Him our hearts in true worship: He has commanded that we all worship Him every Sunday and Holy Day of Obligation by attending Holy Mass and by keeping the Lord's Day holy. The Gift of Piety will help us to remember this every Sunday and Holy Day of our lives.

We also honor God by reverencing the things that pertain to God as "sacred." Proper respect in church, especially in the Presence of Jesus in the Blessed Sacrament, as well as honoring any objects that have been blessed, are beautiful ways to express this reverence.

God is pleased by other pious practices that bring our hearts closer to Him, such as making a daily Morning Offering and Examination of Conscience each night, saying other prayers such as the Holy Rosary or Divine Mercy Chaplet, making a Holy Hour with Jesus in the Blessed Sacrament, reading the Bible or other books written by holy men and women, and bringing our hearts to God in quiet meditation or contemplation so that we may form a personal bond with God, who waits for us to knock on that door so that He can open it and welcome us into the Love of the Holy Trinity.

By extension, Piety teaches us how to fulfill our duties to others. The Holy Spirit's Gift prompts us to remember our proper relationship to our parents, children, and extended families, as well as friends, neighbors, and all those in need. The sincerely pious person is like the Samaritan who saw *himself* in the man who had been robbed and left lying by the side of the road, beaten and bleeding: he knew that, if the same thing had happened to him, he would have hoped for someone to come along who would care for him—bind his wounds, take him to safe shelter, and attend to his physical needs. The Samaritan gave, not from a need to demonstrate generosity, but from a sense of the common bond that all men share in their duty to treat others as they would want to be treated. The widow who gave her two mites is another example—she gave all that she had because she knew there were others who needed that money even more than she. She acted with Piety because she understood how she fit into the bigger picture—in her relationship to God, to others, and to herself.

This painting of the virtue "Pietas," made prior to 1626, is intended to show the classical understanding of this virtue. In ancient Rome, piety was highly valued. Reverence for duty included the proper respect for their gods, as shown by the flaming altar of sacrifice that "Pietas" is holding. Piety also involved great devotion to one's family. The stork pictured here is a reference to filial piety. When parent storks grow too old to provide for themselves, their adult children feed and care for their parents, even carrying them in flight on their backs. In Hebrew, the word for stork, "chasida," stands for piety.

(Cf. "Stork," Watson's Biblical and Theological Dictionary at www.studylight.org).

"Pietas." Alleyn Bequest, 1626. Public Domain.

Widow's Mite. 100BC. PD.

The Seven Gifts of the Holy Spirit
FEAR OF THE LORD

Fear is not always a bad thing. Fear can make us more aware of what is important. Fear can motivate us to do what we need to do. But the Gift of the Holy Spirit called "Fear of the Lord" is not about being afraid of God; it is a kind of holy fear that helps us become aware of who God is and who we are in comparison.

When we realize that God is All-Good, All-Powerful, All-Knowing, then we begin to see how small and imperfect we are. We understand our true place in the universe. Our holy fear of God is a type of awe and wonder that acknowledges with joy His total Power and Majesty. If we ponder God's creation—the size of the universe, the intricacy of an atom, the beauty of a flower, the miracle of a newborn baby—how can we not give Glory to God, who in His awesome Power made all that is good? When we listen to the promptings of the Holy Spirit in the Gift of Fear of the Lord, this holy fear brings us closer to God and helps us understand who we really are.

Moses covers his face in the Presence of God. Burning Bush, by Sébastien Bourdon, 17th c. Public Domain.

Fear of the Lord is the beginning of wisdom.
—*Proverbs 9: 10*

There is another aspect to this Gift of Fear of the Lord. Once we ponder how wonderful God is, then we strive through the inspiration of the Holy Spirit to remain holy in God's sight to protect our friendship with Him. In this way, the Gift of Fear of the Lord helps us guard our souls from sin so we can nurture a loving relationship with God.

When Moses approached God in the Burning Bush, he covered his head in holy fear. Moses asked God His Name, and God replied, "I Am Who Am"—I am Being Itself.

The Holy Trinity and Heavenly Court. St. Benedict, Terre Haute, IN. ©Nheyob, 2011. CC BY SA 3.0.

The Seven Catholic Virtues

www.catholiclibrary.org. Public Domain.

THE THREE **THEOLOGICAL** VIRTUES
FAITH, HOPE, LOVE

The word *theological* refers to the knowledge of God. The graces, or gifts of God, by which we believe in Him, hope in Him, and love Him, are called the theological virtues because they come from God to help us to arrive at a knowledge of God—something we could not achieve without His Divine Graces. Saint Paul tells us: "*Faith, hope, and love abide, these three; and the greatest of these is love*" (*1 Cor. 13: 13*).

THE FOUR **CARDINAL** VIRTUES
JUSTICE, PRUDENCE, TEMPERANCE, FORTITUDE

Human nature is endowed with four natural virtues, which we call the Cardinal Virtues. All of us have varying amounts of them. Some are courageous, some wise, some exercise a clear sense of justice, some are cautious in acting after thinking things through. These virtues need to be cultivated by habits that incline us to making good choices and following through on them.

The Theological Virtues: FAITH

Jesus is transfigured in light as Abraham & Elijah confer with Him. Peter, James, and John witness this Divine moment. The Transfiguration of Jesus, by Pietro Perugina, circa 1500. Public Domain.

Virtues are ways of thinking and acting that help us to be better people. By practicing the virtues, we learn better ways to get along with each other, to be happy with our state in life, to accept the sad times, and to keep on going. This helps us to be more pleasing to God, Who is All-Perfect, All-Good, and All-Loving. He wants us to be perfected in Him so that we can be with Him, but He knows how hard this is for us!

For this reason, God gives us special assistance in addition to the Cardinal Virtues—which are the virtues we can develop through our natural human abilities. God gives us special graces beyond our human abilities, graces flowing from His own Divine Life. These special virtues are *super*natural because we cannot acquire them by our natural efforts. The supernatural virtues are called "theological" because they come directly from God.

When we were baptized, we received the Theological Virtues of Faith, Hope, and Love. Even though they are gifts, we still need to work at practicing these virtues because God desires that we <u>freely choose</u> to believe in Him, to love Him, and to want to please Him. God desires that we love Him freely; in order to make this possible, He gives us the ability to make free choices concerning how and when we will love Him and honor Him.

The Theological Virtues give added life to all the virtues that Christians are called to practice. These three virtues are the foundation upon which all moral choices should be made and the means by which the Holy Spirit is able to guide us to do the right thing. In this way, we can make good choices, stay united with God, and keep His grace—His Divine Life—in our souls.

The theological Virtue of Faith gives us the power to believe in God and all He has revealed to us. Our Lord Jesus said, "I Am the Way, the Truth, and the Life" (John 14: 6). Faith is the virtue that helps us see the truth in everything Jesus said and in everything the Church teaches—truths that come from what God has revealed through Jesus. When we come to know the Truth through the virtue of Faith, we strive to follow the Truth and live in the light of Hope and Love. It is hard to separate these three virtues—which work together in our souls to keep us united to God and inspire us to do His Will in all things.

The virtue of Faith is not just about believing in the Truth; it includes the desire to profess our Faith and witness to that Faith—to share it with the world! That is what Jesus meant when He told His disciples to never hide their light under a bushel basket. The Light of the world is not meant to be hidden, just as a candle is not meant to be covered: Faith gives us strength to believe and to shine before the world like a candle that lights the way to the Truth, which is God's Love—this message of Faith, Hope, and Love is what the world needs!

The Theological Virtues: HOPE

The second of the three Theological Virtues is Hope. Hopefulness is a natural attribute; some people tend to look on the "brighter side," while others might not have a disposition that is as sunny by nature. But the theological virtue of Hope is different—it is a special grace given by God to help us live the Christian life well—a *super*natural kind of hope.

It has not always been easy to be a Christian. In certain times in history, Christians have been misunderstood by others, sometimes persecuted, and even put to death because they would not deny God. It is hard to be "sunny" when you are suffering, especially if you are being mistreated. But supernatural Hope helps us to overcome all these obstacles, making it possible for Christians to persevere in Hope in spite of everything. Saint Paul tells us in his Epistle [Letter] to the Hebrews:

We have this as a sure and steadfast anchor of the soul, a hope that enters into the inner shrine behind the curtain, where Jesus has gone as a forerunner on our behalf . . .
(Hebrews 6: 19)

The virtue of hope is much more than a positive attitude about life—it is a special hope for the joys of Heaven, for the blessedness of being with God, for complete peace and joy. Jesus told us in His sermon on the mount:

Blessed are those who hunger and thirst for righteousness, for they shall be satisfied.
(Matthew 5: 6)

The Old Testament Psalms celebrate this hope in God:

Trust in Him at all times . . . God is a refuge for us.
(Psalm 62: 9)
It is better to take refuge in the Lord than to put confidence in man.
(Psalm 118: 8)

Saint Paul describes the use of the Theological Virtues as robing oneself in the armor of God:

Put on the breastplate of faith and love, and for a helmet the hope of salvation.
(1 Thess. 5: 8)

Hope strengthens us to continue to believe in the

Jesus Multiplies the Loaves & Fishes, by F.X. Zettler, 1912. Denver Cathedral. Public Domain.

power of Christ's Resurrection regardless of the struggles and trials of life. Hope helps us to be faithful to God in our thoughts, words, and actions in spite of whatever sufferings and temptations we may encounter. Hope inspires us to continue striving toward our final destin, which is eternal happiness with God in Heaven. Not only that, but the supernatural virtue of Hope instills in us a thirst for the things of God and encourages us to desire union with God and to aim for the joys of Heaven.

With love and trust in Jesus Christ and sure confidence in the power of the Holy Spirit to provide us with the graces we need, we will be able to prevail in this life. If tragedy, sadness, discouragement, loneliness, or pain tug at our hearts, the supernatural virtue of Hope keeps our feet on the sure path that leads us home.

Never hesitate to call on the Holy Spirit to refresh this precious gift of grace in you! Saint Paul tells us there are only three things that last: Faith, Hope, and Love. Yet Hope does not last forever—when we reach that Heavenly goal of being happy with God for all eternity, our Hope will be fulfilled!

THE BOOK OF SEVENS

The Theological Virtues: CHARITY

The Most Holy Trinity: The Throne of Mercy. ©Reinhardhauke, 2010. CC BY-SA 3.0.

The picture above is a stained-glass artist's attempt to show in brilliant light and colors the majestic power of the Love of God. God the Father sent His Only-Begotten Son Jesus Christ, now resurrected from the dead, into the world to save mankind from sin and death. The Holy Spirit, the Sanctifier, showers Divine Graces from the Heart of the Holy Trinity on mankind.

The Virtue of Charity is a supernatural Love that is totally selfless—Love that desires to give rather than receive—the way God loves. God's Nature is a perfect example of Charity, because no one is more generous than God! The sun shines and the rain falls every day on both the good and the bad (Matthew 5: 45). God does not limit His gifts to those who deserve them—but showers His Saving Love on everyone.

Jesus told a parable about a master who sent servants to his vineyard to collect his grapes from his workers. Instead, the workers beat the servants; the workers wanted to keep the grapes for themselves! The master tried everything to help the workers to do the right thing. He sent his only beloved son to them, thinking, "Surely they will respect my son." But the workers killed him (Mark 12: 1-9). Just so, God the Father sent His only Son Jesus into the world to save mankind, even though He knew that Jesus would be rejected and put to death on the Cross! God gave the greatest gift of all, the Gift of His Beloved Son: through Christ we receive forgiveness for our sins and gain life everlasting in Heaven. This is the wonder of God's merciful love for us!

God gives us the freedom to love Him, but He does not force us. At Baptism, He gives us the three Theological Virtues, most especially the Virtue of Charity, the gifts of His grace to help us choose to be united with God so we can enjoy eternal life with Him in Heaven.

Because all that we are and all that we have come from God's generous love, we cannot love Him with the same completely selfless love with which He has loved us. But when we love others with true Charity, that is our way of showing God that we love Him with the kind of generosity He has shown us. "Forgive us our trespasses as we forgive those who trespass against us" means asking God to love us in the same measure that we love others.

As Saint Paul said, "So faith, hope, love abide, but the greatest of these is love" (1 Cor. 13: 13). True Charity will last forever.

The Cardinal Virtues: JUSTICE

As the saying goes, "Practice makes perfect." Virtues are habits that we practice in life in order to be more perfect—to be good people, to help make the world a better place for everyone, and to be pleasing to God, who is the Source of all our truest joys. As Saint Augustine once said, "Our hearts are restless, Lord, until they rest in Thee."

Habits take work. Just as faithful devotion to exercise is required to build muscles, the Cardinal Virtues require devoted effort to become effective in the way we live and the choices we make. Human beings are born with a sense of four basic virtues called the *Cardinal* Virtues: Prudence, Justice, Fortitude, and Temperance. These natural tendencies can be suppressed or nurtured, but they are basic to human experience and part of the way that people interact in society. The easiest of the Cardinal Virtues to begin with is Justice.

Justice is often pictured as an Angel holding a large scale that should be perfectly balanced. This image of the concept of Justice expresses without words a sense of fairness that is common to every human person. Everyone, even a young child, can recognize if things are not fair—cheating, stealing, or even reserving the best for one's self—these are examples of ways that individuals seek to take what is not rightfully theirs. Justice is imbalanced when people are treated unfairly by others—when people are burdened with greater punishments than others who have committed the same crimes or when people are limited to less than they deserve because they are being persecuted. These are crimes against justice. When the scale becomes imbalanced, then it must be righted again.

On the level of social interaction and nations, many wars and atrocities can be traced back to these imbalanced scales. On the personal level, many divorces, broken homes, and other tragedies can sometimes be boiled down to some initial injustice that was never righted. It is easy to see that practicing the Virtue of Justice is extremely important, both to individuals and to the world: world peace begins with each human heart.

Justice is that habit of Virtue that balances what is deserved, what is rightful, what is fair, for each person. But Justice can be tricky. Equality of parts is not always justice, because sometimes one person may deserve more or less than another. Justice works best when tempered with the other Cardinal Virtues, which will be discussed later.

One example of the wisdom needed to practice the Virtue of Justice comes from the life of King Solomon. As Job said, "I was clad with justice: and I clothed myself with my judgment, as with a robe and a diadem" (*Job 29: 14*). Solomon's justice was perfected in his judgment of what each person deserved in true fairness. As the King of Israel, he sat in judgment over cases that required his judgment. One such case was particularly thorny: two mothers both claimed the same newborn son as her own. No one could tell which woman was the true mother, so King Solomon ordered the child to be cut in two so that each woman would have an equal portion. Immediately, one of the women backed down, saying the she was not the true mother. But Solomon knew that she

Solomon's Wisdom Finds the True Mother. Musée de Lille. Released to Public Domain by Vassil, 2008.

protested because she <u>was</u> the true mother and cared more about saving her baby's life than did the other woman, who only wanted the child out of jealousy because she had lost her own baby.

While justice between persons is often decided using the legal system, this is not the primary exercise of the Virtue of Justice on the level of the Christian. Jesus advises us to settle our differences before even arriving at court. He challenges us to temper Justice with Mercy:

> *But I say to you: Love your enemies and pray for those who persecute you, so that you may be sons of your Father who is in Heaven; for He makes His sun to rise on the evil and on the good, and sends rain on the just and on the unjust.* (Matthew 5: 44-45)

Justice practiced with respect for others and their property leads to peace: "The fruit of justice is sown in peace, to them that make peace" (*James 3: 18*).

The Cardinal Virtues: PRUDENCE

Christ in the House of Martha & Mary, by Jan Vermeer, c1656. Public Domain.

The Virtue of Prudence is the power to use reason before acting and then choose the best action. Thought to be the most important virtue by the philosophers, it was called the "charioteer of the virtues" because it leads all the other virtues to the right outcomes. For example, Fortitude [*courage*] turns into sheer folly if a person decides to be courageous at the wrong time! Justice can become unjust if a person chooses to apply the wrong standard in trying to make a good judgment.

The word "prudence" has a limited connotation in modern usage—today the word means to be cautious or careful, especially with regard to financial matters. But prudence as a virtue uses the classical definition of the word, which, in modern usage, translates to "rational discernment." In light of this, the virtue of prudence is seen as the ability to consider the possible outcomes of actions before performing them and then discerning which actions are the best before acting.

Knowing the difference between right and wrong is essential to forming a good conscience. When questions arise about what the best course of action might be, the mind can distinguish which actions are good and which are not. When the mind makes this distinction, then the habit of prudence guides the mind to choose those actions which are good.

A well-formed conscience provides one with the knowledge to weigh actions not only in terms of good and evil, but also in the context of each specific situation. This kind of knowledge is also called *insight* or *wisdom*. The Old Testament contains an entire section called "Wisdom Literature" filled with advice about how to cultivate Prudence, including: Job, Psalms, Proverbs, Ecclesiastes, the Canticle of Canticles, Wisdom, and Ecclesiasticus.

One example of Prudence comes from the New Testament. Jesus went to visit His good friends who lived in Bethany: Lazarus and his sisters Martha and Mary. Because Jesus was their honored guest, they were preparing a special dinner for Him. Martha was working hard to get everything ready—cooking, cleaning, setting the table. But Mary was not helping at all. Instead, she sat on a footstool at Jesus' feet, listening to His every word. Martha was impatient with her sister and upbraided Mary in front of Jesus for not helping her. When Jesus heard Martha's rebuke, He reprimanded Martha, saying,

> "Martha, Martha, you are worried and distracted by many things; there is need of only one thing. Mary has chosen the better part, which will not be taken away from her."
> *(Luke 10: 41-42)*

Mary's choice to learn from Jesus was more prudent than Martha's, who focused on a lesser good than the one Mary chose.

> **Fear of the Lord is the beginning of wisdom: and the knowledge of the holy is prudence.**
> *(Proverbs 9: 10)*

The Cardinal Virtues: TEMPERANCE

Temperance is the Virtue that helps people to gain mastery over their desires and appetites. All human beings have physical and emotional needs that are good in themselves but still require moderation. Too little or too much of a good thing is not good and can lead to grave evils for the person who does not gain mastery over self, as well as for the other people who may be affected by that person's lack of temperance. This is why regular practice of the Virtue of Temperance is crucial. It is never easy to master self-restraint, but with vigilance comes strength of resolve.

The Accolade by Edmund Blair Leighton. Public Domain.

In the Middle Ages, it was customary for a young man to keep vigil all night long before Jesus in the Tabernacle while holding his sword before becoming a knight. Being dubbed with his sword meant that the knight promised to fight for the right and protect the weak and helpless. Only through Temperance could he do so.

Justice and Prudence are focused on the power of the mind, first, to know what is fair and, second, to discern how to act on that knowledge. Temperance focuses on the will. What is required here is the will power to say "no" to appetites and desires that may have great attraction for us but may do us harm. Jesus warns: "*Watch and pray that you may not enter into temptation; the spirit indeed is willing, but the flesh is weak*" (Mark 14: 38).

Moderation is key to controlling our appetites; it can be good for the body and pleasant for the senses to eat and drink, but eating either too little or too much is not good for the body or spirit. Having a loving relationship with a married spouse is good and beautiful, but entering into a marital relationship with someone who is not one's spouse is against God's laws. As with any pleasure in life, be it a physical or emotional attraction or drive, the virtue of Temperance keeps natural impulses from taking over.

The same is true for faults—such as a quick temper or an addiction—which need to be mastered so they do not take over, causing the person to say or do things they would not do if they were in full control of their emotions and impulses.

The need to work at Temperance is one reason why the Church established laws of fasting and abstinence on specific days in Lent. Practicing self-mastery when it is not a personal necessity is a great way to flex willpower muscles! Offering up these efforts to master appetites and desires as a sacrifice in honor of Christ's Sacrifice adds even greater value to such opportunities: "*If any man would come after Me, let him deny himself and take up his cross and follow Me*" (Matthew 17: 24). As one of the four Cardinal Virtues, Temperance helps with Prudence, Justice, and Fortitude to each be more effective in their own capacities.

The Cardinal Virtues: FORTITUDE

Sir Thomas More and Bishop John Fisher, Saints. English School of Painting, 1600s. Public Domain.

These men were among the most powerful in England during the difficult reign of King Henry VIII. Thomas More was the Lord Chancellor and John Fisher was the Cardinal-Bishop of the Diocese of Rochester. Both men refused to give in when the King decided to break with the Catholic Church by naming himself (and not the Pope) as Head of the Church in England. In 1535, both men were beheaded for their stand supporting the Catholic Church as the one true Church established by Christ & headed only by successors of St. Peter.

Fortitude is the habit of Virtue that steels the will to do the right thing, even when the mind has good reasons to argue against it. Temperance uses willpower to master desires and emotions; fortitude works to control the mind when doing the right thing might not be the safer course of action! Going into battle is a good example of suppressing the mind's best instincts for survival—every soldier knows that he faces sure dangers and possibly injury or death. Yet fortitude gives him power to conquer those instincts for the sake of a greater purpose—to protect his country and those he loves.

A powerful example of fortitude in the face of political, social ruin and even death is the witness of both Saint Thomas More and Saint John Fisher. Both were among the most powerful in England under King Henry VIII. But both men refused to betray their faith in God and their allegiance to the Catholic Church. Both paid for this unpopular stand with their careers, their fortunes, and their lives.

When Henry's older brother Arthur died after marrying the Spanish princess Catherine of Aragon, Henry received a Papal dispensation to marry her himself. But during a marriage of over 20 years, all their children had died at birth or soon after, except

for Mary Tudor. Henry contended that God was punishing him by not giving him a son (even as his roving eye lighted on lady-in-waiting Ann Boleyn). Henry demanded a new dispensation from the Pope to divorce Catherine and marry Ann. Because the first dispensation was still binding, the Pope refused. Henry, who had once presented himself as "Defender of the Faith," broke with the Catholic Church, declared himself head of the church in England, divorced Catherine, and married Ann Boleyn.

All the Catholic Bishops in England acquiesced to the King's will except for Bishop John Fisher, who preached publicly that Saint Peter and his successor Popes are the only ones ordained by Christ to be heads of His Church. Thomas More resigned as Chancellor of England, losing his power and prestige and retiring to his country home. Both men refused to take the oath that everyone in England was then required to take in which they swore that the King, not the Pope, was head of the church. Both ended up imprisoned in the Tower of London. When neither would give lip service to the King's demands, Henry VIII ordered their execution. Both men were beheaded on Tower Hill in the summer of 1535. Their fortitude helped them witness to the truth.

The Virtue of CHASTITY

Gianna Beretta Molla is a great example of a modern woman who balanced her professional career with her role as wife and mother. Born in 1922 in Magenta, Italy, she entered medical school in Milan in 1942; in 1949, near her hometown, she opened her own practice specializing in pediatrics. She had hoped that one day she would be able to join her brother, a priest in Brazil, and serve the poor women there with gynecological care, but her own fragile health proved that such a mission would be impossible.

In December 1954, she met Pietro Mollo, an engineer, and fell in love. Engaged the following April, they married in September 1955. The couple were blessed with three children: Pierluigi (1956), Mariolina (1957), Laura (1959), but then Gianna suffered two miscarriages. In the second month of her sixth pregnancy, doctors discovered complications resulting from a fibroma of the uterus. They recommended one of three options: an abortion, a hysterectomy, or uterine surgery to remove the fibroid. Abortion is not ever considered an acceptable option by the Church, even in cases where the mother's life is endangered. But a hysterectomy would not have been considered morally wrong, because the reason for the surgery in that case would not be to *cause* the baby's death, but would be an "unintended consequence" of a treatment that was specifically to save the life of the mother. Despite the fact that Gianna could have chosen the

Saint Gianna Beretta Molla. ©José Luiz Bernardes Riberio, 2014. CC BY-SA 3.0.

morally acceptable option to have a hysterectomy, she chose to have only fibroid surgery—because she wanted to save her baby, even if it meant endangering her own life. After a very difficult pregnancy, she delivered Gianna Emanuela on Good Friday, 1962, but died seven days later of septic peritonitis.

When Gianna was named a Saint by Pope John Paul II in 2004, it was the first time in history that a Saint's husband had ever attended his wife's canonization. As a beautiful example of chastity in marriage, in motherhood, and in her career as a physician, Gianna, who loved selflessly with purity of both body and soul, once said:

"Our body is a cenacle, a monstrance: through its crystal the world should see God."

---

www.coronaerosarum.com   THE BOOK OF SEVENS

The Virtue of PIETY

St. Rose of Lima Adores the Christ Child with tender piety, by Murillo. Public Domain.

Piety is the habit of Virtue that teaches us to treat God with the reverence and love that is due to Him as our Creator and Savior. When we contemplate the wonders of God—His Power, Beauty, Truth, and Goodness—we come to realize how much He truly deserves our respect. When we consider how small we are in comparison to God, it becomes even more clear that the proper way to respond to God's Love is with love, adoration, praise, and thanksgiving.

The picture above shows Saint Rose of Lima wearing the habit of a Third Order Dominican. Rose was very close to God and spent most of her time praying and doing penances to show her love. She stands over Baby Jesus, who has just appeared to her and offers her a rose. She looks down at Our Lord with tender love and deep respect. Her way of responding to the love that Jesus offers her demonstrates the virtue of Piety.

In the same way, we show the virtue of Piety whenever we genuflect to Jesus Present in the Tabernacle as we enter and leave the pew, when we stand up for the reading of the Gospel during Mass, when we bow or make another gesture of reverence before receiving Holy Communion, and when we fold our hands together as we pray. These outward physical signs give honor and glory to God as we love, adore, and praise Him inwardly with our hearts and minds.

God is ever faithful to us, even if we forget His Love and generosity. He created us and blesses us with all the good gifts around us. We should always strive to be faithful to God with true Piety.

God has commanded that we give Him the worship He deserves by attending Holy Mass every Sunday and Holy Day of Obligation. He made us His adopted children in Jesus Christ through the Sacrament of Baptism, so we should always try to devote ourselves to loving Him by practicing the virtue of Piety, unafraid to show our reverence and love for God.

God Created the Sun and Moon, by Michelangelo. The Sistine Chapel, the Vatican. Public Domain.

The Seven Heavenly Virtues:
Conquer the Seven Deadly Sins!

Virtues are ways of thinking and acting that help us to choose to be better people. Virtues are habits that, when practiced and cultivated, help us to build up the moral, spiritual, and even physical strength to choose good over evil, to avoid temptation, and to remain faithful to God and His Holy Will. By practicing virtues, we learn better ways to get along with each other, to be happy with our state in life, to accept the sad times and keep on going. This helps us be more pleasing to God, Who is All-Perfect, All-Good, and All-Loving.

God wants us to be perfected in Him so we can be with Him, but He knows how hard this is for us! For this reason, He gives us a share in His own Divine Life, what we call "graces," to help us in our struggle to be good. As long as we are able to receive these graces, God walks with us, supports us when we struggle, lifts us up when we fall, and helps us to reach our goals in this life and in the next—the goal of reaching Heaven is to be united with God in the Beatific Vision, which is eternal happiness.

Sadly, there are choices we make that can separate us from God and from the life of grace. These choices are called sins; the most serious sins are called "Mortal" sins because they cut us off from the life of grace and separate us from the Love of God.

At the close of the 4th century, a man named Aurelius Clemens Prudentius, a holy Christian, wrote a book called *The Battle of the Soul*. In his book, Prudentius described the struggle to make good choices and avoid making bad choices that can separate us from God. He named seven specific choices that are so serious that they separate us from the Love of God. He called these bad choices the *Seven Deadly Sins*. He also named *Seven Heavenly Virtues*, which are good choices we can make that help us preserve our union with God and receive His life-giving graces.

This chapter focuses on these *Seven Heavenly Virtues*. Each page describes one of these virtues and how the practice of that virtue assists in avoiding the bad choices that lead to the *Seven Deadly Sins*.

By practicing the *Seven Heavenly Virtues,* you can strengthen your will, heart, mind, and soul to choose what is good and reject what is evil.

The Seven Heavenly Virtues Defeat the Seven Deadly Sins!

✠ **Humility conquers Pride**
✠ **Temperance curtails Gluttony**
✠ **Charity overwhelms Greed**
✠ **Kindness neutralizes Envy**
✠ **Chastity protects against Lust**
✠ **Patience soothes Anger**
✠ **Diligence drives away Sloth**

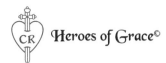
The Heavenly Virtue of Humility

The Heavenly Virtue of Humility is not an easy virtue to describe. The word *humility* is sometimes associated with something inferior, such as someone of "humble birth"—meaning one who is born into impoverished circumstances. Another use of the word *humility* involves being humiliated—"eating humble pie," so to speak. However, these connotations of the word *humility* do not pertain to the Virtue. Humility as a Virtue is a type of modesty or restraint that comes from seeing one's self in the light of truth.

It may be easier to start by saying what the Virtue of Humility is not! The opposite of the Virtue of Humility is the Deadly Sin of Pride. Pride comes in many forms: vainglory, vanity, selfishness, conceit, arrogance, snobbery, narcissism—all vices that stem from a love of self that is not truthful.

The sin of Pride kicks in when we compare ourselves to others—and decide we are better than others and should come first. A proud person takes the best seat or the nicest slice of cake or the first place in line. Such a person wants to be the center of attention, to "show off," even to pushing other people out of the way. It does not really matter to a proud person if the one being pushed aside is actually more deserving or more unselfish!

The person who practices the Virtue of Humility does just the opposite of the proud person—a truly humble person gives the best seat to someone else, takes the burnt slice of toast so someone else can have the nicer one, and draws everyone's attention to the accomplishments and good qualities of another rather than trying to grasp at admiration for one's self. A truly humble person can bring so much goodness and joy into the world!

Humility is always based on the truth. It is not about pretending to be something that you are not. Some of the greatest Saints, such as Saint Thérèse of Lisieux, practiced the Virtue of Humility. They did not deny their own goodness, but neither did they exaggerate it or allow it to blur their ability to see themselves as they really were—to appreciate the goodness in themselves, even as they freely admitted their faults.

Just as pride is the root of many forms of evil, Humility is the wellspring from which many other Virtues can grow. For example, Humility helps build the Virtue of Temperance because it teaches us to govern our own desires by denying the instinct to

St. Augustine Contemplates the Truths of God, by Sandro Botticelli, 1480. Public Domain.

push ahead of others or take the best for ourselves.

Practicing the Virtue of Humility is at the heart of the struggle to master the self. Saint Augustine understood many deep truths about God and the life of the soul; he many wrote books on philosophy and theology that are still studied today—more than 1,600 years later. He was once asked, "Which are the three greatest virtues?" Saint Augustine replied quietly, "Humility, humility, humility."

Try to imagine what Heaven will be like, where there will be no vain pride, jealousy, or selfishness. We will look at each other and rejoice, praising God for the good and beautiful gifts that others have— that we don't! We will give and receive praise with complete peace and joy for the good things with which God in His Wisdom has blessed each of us. We will see each other "as we truly are" and know that God, who is the Source of all beauty and truth, loves a truly humble heart.

The Heavenly Virtue of Temperance

Like the Virtue of Humility, the Heavenly Virtue of Temperance helps to support all the other virtues. Temperance helps us to achieve a greater control over the will, the emotions, and the appetites and, therefore, makes it possible for us to achieve mastery over the self. Temperance helps to weigh and measure what is appropriate and to moderate our desires accordingly. When we learn to control our desires, we can find the strength necessary to resist temptations to those things that we know are not good or virtuous.

Learning to control oneself requires lifelong effort. It is ESPECIALLY important for young people—adolescents and young adults—to learn these skills. There will be many occasions as one grows from childhood to maturity to give into many kinds of desires that may seem good in themselves—food, drink, worldly pleasures and creature comforts, success, fortune, power, fame, and even spiritual gifts. But, if these desires take over—rather than the will remaining in control of the situation—the result can be like a run-away train that even can lead to sins that one may not have wanted to commit!

It is far better to prepare in advance rather than allow the lack of Temperance to leave open that door to temptation. Think of Temperance as a wall surrounding a castle, protecting it from sudden invasion. Every time we say "no" to something we may want to do or to have—but that we know may not be good for us at that time, we add another brick to that wall and make it stronger. The Saints sometimes gave up things that WERE good for them, like basic meals or shoes or sleep, in order to strengthen their wills. To exercise the will in this way is like exercising a muscle—the more we do it, the stronger it gets.

Gluttony is the Deadly Sin that is destroyed by the Virtue of Temperance, which builds self-discipline. Through Temperance, one learns to make good choices when responding to one's desires. Temperance teaches a person what is appropriate and judicious for each occasion, such as, when to stop eating. At a banquet, many wonderful foods delight the eye and taste buds. The ancient Romans used to eat too much food because they were enjoying the sheer pleasure of

The Virtue of Temperance, by Lorenzetti, 1340. Detail from The Allegory of Good Government. Fresco at the Public Palace, Siena. Public Domain.

eating. However, too much is not good for the body and leads to terrible excesses such as gluttony, drunkenness, obesity, sloth, and waste. All those vices could be avoided by simply knowing when to push one's self away from the table. Temperance helps us to balance our desires with what we know to be the right thing to do. But that takes real will power, and will power is achieved by the virtuous habit of self-discipline.

Temperance helps us to see beyond the moment and beyond the gratification of each desire, to help us realize that every good gift God gives us to enjoy should be used for a good purpose—health, safety, beauty, joy, love. All the things that give Glory to God lead us to ultimate happiness in Heaven. An of the things that are harmful to ourselves or to others are NOT good choices. Those harmful things should be avoided—even when our natural desires tend to pull us toward them.

The Heavenly Virtue of Charity

The Parable of the Good Samaritan, by Giacomo Conti, 18th century. Public Domain.

The Heavenly Virtue of Charity is much more than making a charitable donation to the needy. True Charity is the rock upon which all the virtues are built. Saint Paul tells us that, should we give away all that we own or move mountains, speak in the language of the angels or even understand all the mysteries of God, "but have not love," we are no more than "a noisy gong or a clanging symbol." He even says that, without love, we are nothing, and we gain nothing by our good works (1 Cor. 13 : 1-3).

The Pharisees practiced many virtues (especially in public) and followed all the strict Mosaic Laws with devotion, but they were motivated by pride, not by love. Jesus called them "whitened sepulchers" (Matt. 23: 27)—beautifully painted white coffins full of "dead men's bones and every kind of filth."

Saint Augustine teaches that there are two kinds of love: *caritas*, "charity," and *cupiditas*, "selfish love." *Caritas* [*the Latin word that "charity" comes from*] is a kind of love that seeks to share, to help others, to give freely, and to give all the Glory to God. This is the way that God loves us.

The other kind of love, *cupiditas*, is a type of love that seeks to take rather than give, to gratify one's own desires, to put one's own needs before the good of others. The Deadly Sin that opposes the Heavenly Virtue of Charity is Greed. Greed can take many forms, from trying to hoard good things for yourself, to giving to others only when you know you will get something in return. It is not good enough to do someone a kindness in order to be well thought of or to get something in return. *Caritas* is a generosity of spirit that does not look at "what's in it for me," but gives out of a love that does not limit itself.

Jesus told a parable about a man who was robbed, beaten, and left to die by the side of the road. Several people passed by but no one stopped to help—until a Samaritan came by. In those days, the Jews did not like Samaritans; they would not even speak to them. But this Samaritan saw a Jew in need and showed him true charity, dressing his wounds, carrying him to an inn, and paying the innkeeper to care for the man. He did not help with any expectation of repayment; he helped out of pure charity.

Jesus told another parable about a master who sent his servants to his vineyard to collect his grapes from the workers. After his servants were beaten or killed by the workers, the master sent his "beloved son," thinking "they will respect my son." But the workers murdered his son, too! (Mark 12: 1-9). In actuality, God sent His only Son into the world at Christmas to save the world, knowing that Jesus would be rejected and put to death on the Cross! God loved us so much that He was still willing to send His Beloved Son to save us.

The perfect example of Charity is God: no one is more generous than He! The sun shines and rain falls every day on both the good and the bad (Matt. 5: 45). God does not limit His gifts to the deserving but showers His Love on all.

The true meaning of giving gifts at Christmas is this gift, the Gift that God gave the world when He sent His Beloved Son into the world that night two thousand years ago in Bethlehem, so that we could have freedom from death and enjoy life everlasting in Heaven! ***We are called to love others in the same way that God has loved us!***

The Heavenly Virtue of Kindness

The Heavenly Virtue of Kindness has been given many names: Empathy, Trust, Compassion, Cheerfulness, Caring. These are all words that attempt to describe the practice of being good to others without harboring resentment or prejudice—what Shakespeare called "the milk of human kindness." Those who are truly kind give to others from a generosity that does not make comparisons or set limits.

By contrast, the Deadly Sin that opposes the Heavenly Virtue of Kindness is Envy. Envy compares, envy desires, envy resents what others have. Rather than opening up one's heart to the needs and true welfare of others, envy narrows the scope of the heart to the self. In medieval iconography, Envy was pictured as a woman with a serpent coiled around her biting her heart, as she gnaws at her own hand in bitterness. It is interesting to note that the ancient Greek goddess of Envy was named Nemesis.

The Virtue of Kindness, when nurtured, bears beautiful spiritual fruit in the person who learns to practice it, as well as bringing joy to all those who have the good fortune to know such a person. To make friends with such a person is one of life's greatest gifts. A person who truly cares for others without making distinctions brings peace to the world, heals wounds, and even helps restore the order that God ordained for mankind before the Fall of Adam and Eve.

The picture at right is one artist's effort to show visually the beauty and power of true Kindness. Not only does the man who embraces Christ show deep sympathy for sufferings that Christ endured on the Cross for us, he has taken up a cross of his own, carrying it out of love for Jesus and giving himself over completely to sharing in the sufferings of the Beloved One.

Only when the world learns to remove Envy from human experience will mankind be able to truly "love one another."

Compassion, by William-Adolphe Bouguereau, 1897. Public Domain.

www.coronaerosarum.com   THE BOOK OF SEVENS

The Heavenly Virtue of Chastity

The Heavenly Virtue of Chastity builds upon a view of the self and of others that respects the dignity of every human being. To be chaste is to recognize the immense value of your person, your soul, and your physical body, as well as the value of other people, too. We are each a special creation, made by God to know Him, love Him, and serve Him, so we can be happy with Him forever in Heaven. This is our true destiny.

When you see yourself and other people in this way, you see that every child of God should be treated with love and respect. A person should never be treated as the object of another person's pleasure. About 100 years ago, a girl named Maria lived with her mother and siblings on a farm in Italy. After Maria's father died, her mother had to take on male boarders to help tend the farm. Giovanni and Alessandro Serenelli, father and son, lived under the same roof and ate with her family. Alessandro was a moody 17-year-old who stayed in his room when he was not in the fields.

One day when everyone else was in the fields except Alessandro, who was in his room, Maria was cooking dinner. The boy came out of his room and made an unchaste suggestion to Maria. Maria was only 11 years old and had just made her First Holy Communion. She refused the boy's advances. In violent anger, Alessandro picked up a kitchen knife and stabbed Maria repeatedly. Maria died the next day, forgiving Alessandro for his cruelty to her and praying for his soul, which she knew was in danger. She knew that he kept to his room because the walls were covered with pornography. Alessandro had allowed this vice to take over his life and cloud his judgment. He spent most of his life in prison paying for his crime, angry and bitter, until Maria appeared to him in a dream and gave him a lily for each of the wounds he given her with the knife.

Alessandro realized that he had given in to the sin of Lust, which is the Deadly Sin that opposes the Heavenly Virtue of Chastity. He had used other people as objects of his own pleasure, rather than valuing them for the God-given dignity that each human being possesses. After being released

Saint Maria Goretti. Public Domain.

from prison, he became a holy monk, dedicating the rest of his life to atoning for what he had done.

The Virtue of Chastity involves self-control. To keep one's mind and body in check is to learn to say no to those impulses which we know can lead to physical impurity, intoxication, or excessive desires for any kind of pleasure. God gives us the good things that are pleasing to our senses to enjoy, but in moderation and in the right context. In the end, unless we learn to exercise the Virtue of Chastity and resist temptations to impurity, we lose control of ourselves and are unable to enjoy the good gifts that God desires to give us.

In Dante's *Inferno*, souls who did not repent of the sin of Lust occupy a place in Hell where the wind of their passions blows them around forever.

The Heavenly Virtue of Patience

The Heavenly Virtue of Patience is the self control that teaches us to restrain whatever passions may be hurtful or destructive. Patience is like the brakes on the car of our passions; when we see ice ahead, we apply the brakes to slow down so the car does not lose control and crash. We use the brakes to stop at a red light because we know that is the law—a law created to keep everyone safe. The Virtue of Patience works in much the same way. Patience applies the brakes to anger, impatience, selfishness, or the temptation to do something destructive.

Patience reminds us to stop, catch our breath, and think about what is right and wrong before doing something we would regret. Patience is a balancing act between how we might feel and what we should do or not do about it.

The Deadly Sin that opposes the Heavenly Virtue of Patience is Anger. Anger is a sin that not only can lead to hurting others but also hurts the person who allows anger to take hold of their heart and soul. Anger is like a cancer that eats the soul up, turning it into an engine of hatred and revenge that will destroy both the victim and the aggressor.

The Virtue of Patience goes deeper than just restraining our passions. True Patience includes the ability to forgive. It is one thing to keep from hurting others by "applying the brakes" on the passions. But that does not resolve the underlying pain that caused the anger. It does not heal the wounds left open when we are hurt. Not only does Patience require that we accept suffering when it is brought on us by the actions of others, it urges us to be merciful. Only with mercy can there be peace. Peace in hearts and souls. Peace among people. Peace that refuses to give in to wars and violence and cruelty.

All of us are flawed human beings. We have accidents. We make mistakes. We can even do things that are really sinful—and sin is always hurtful to someone, especially to God, who loves us with a mercy greater than we can imagine. Patience teaches us to forgive each other:

***Forgive us our trespasses
as we forgive those who trespass against us.***

The artist Dosso Dossi has put into visual language the terrible force of Anger as it affects the human spirit, causing violence, hatred, confusion, and evil passions.

*The Tussle, 1516.
Collezione Vittorio Cini,
Venice.
Public Domain.*

THE BOOK OF SEVENS

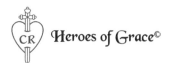
The Heavenly Virtue of Diligence

The word diligence is from a Latin that means "loving what you do." To be diligent is to apply yourself to a task with care and to keep working until it is completed. The Heavenly Virtue of Diligence elevates the idea of hard work to a higher level.

Loving what you do, trying to do it well, taking pride in what you can accomplish, are all good—as long as you keep your ultimate goals in sight. Working hard for the right reason and never losing heart are the habits achieved using the Heavenly Virtue of Diligence.

Jesus told a parable about a master who was going on a journey. Before he left, he gave three servants a task to complete in his absence. He gave each a sum of money and told them to take good care of it while he was away. To one he gave five talents [*a certain measure of gold*], to the second he gave two talents, and to the third he gave one talent, each according to their native ability. The first servant took the five talents and made some

Parable of the Talents, by Andrey Mironov. ©Andrey Mironov, 2013. CC BY-SA 3.0.

very profitable deals, earning five more talents. The second did likewise with his two talents, earning two more. But the third servant, who feared the master—and his own failure—buried the one talent in the ground.

When the master returned, he was greatly pleased by the diligence and industry of the two servants who increased his wealth in his absence. When the third servant brought him just one talent, making excuses out of fear of failure, the master was angry, calling the third servant "wicked and slothful" and casting him into the outer darkness.

Jesus is addressing the issue of diligence in this parable—but not to teach the people how to garner more interest on their investments. He is applying these earthly situations to the life of the soul and its eternal destiny. Jesus is certainly encouraging his followers to be diligent—to take what God blesses them with and use it to increase what is good in the world—but He is really speaking to the ultimate goal of Diligence. Immediately following the parable of the talents (Matthew 25: 14-30), Jesus talks about the

Last Judgment, when the Son of Man will sit on His Throne and separate the "goats" from the "sheep"—and His basis for this separation will be which people in life used their talents [*gifts and abilities*] to feed the hungry, clothe the naked, visit the sick and imprisoned, and welcome strangers. God wants us to be diligent—but for a very clear purpose: He wants us to use our talents to love one another as He has loved us.

In light of this ultimate goal, Diligence is more than hard work. The Virtue of Diligence involves applying oneself, without fear of failure, to whatever tasks God sets before you, whether it be doing your homework well and at the right time, caring for the needs of your family, or applying yourself at your job. The Deadly Sin of Sloth is the opposite of Diligence. Laziness is just one aspect of Sloth, which includes fear of failure and the tendency to become apathetic—not caring, being distracted, becoming dormant. "Idle hands are the devil's workshop."

> "The only thing necessary for the triumph of evil is for good men to do nothing."
> —Edmund Burke

The Seven Corporal Works of Mercy

Virtues are ways of thinking and acting that help us to choose to do the right thing. Virtues are habits that, when practiced and cultivated, help us find the moral, spiritual, and physical strength to choose good over evil, to avoid temptation, and to remain faithful to God and His Holy Will. By practicing the Virtues, we learn better ways to get along with each other, to be happy with our state in life, to accept the sad times, and keep on going. This helps us be more pleasing to God, Who is All-Perfect, All-Good, and All-Loving.

God wants us to be perfected in Him so we can be with Him, but He knows how hard this is for us! For this reason, He gives us a share in His own Divine Life, called "sanctifying grace," to help us to be like Him. God also gives us actual graces to help us to avoid sin. God walks with us, supports us when we struggle, lifts us if we fall, and helps us to reach our goal in this life and in the next.

The Corporal Works of Mercy are virtues that are directed toward serving the physical needs of others. "Corporal" means "of the

Corporal Works of Mercy
1. Feed the Hungry
2. Give Drink to the Thirsty
3. Clothe the Naked
4. Shelter the Homeless
5. Visit the Sick
6. Visit the Imprisoned
7. Bury the Dead

body" and refers to ways we can help others with their physical needs. There are also seven "Spiritual" Works of Mercy that help with needs that are not physical—but still very important to those who need Mercy.

This chapter offers a page for each Corporal Work of Mercy. When we know these Works we can begin to practice them, even with our family and friends. In this way, we learn the many ways we can offer Mercy to meet many different peoples' needs. God does not limit His Mercy; He is Merciful to everyone who asks for His Mercy. He asks us to show our gratitude to Him for the gifts He has given us by showing Mercy to others. Remember that when you pray the *Our Father*, you are asking God to measure His Mercy toward you in the same measure that you show Mercy to others: *"Forgive us our trespasses as we forgive those who trespass against us."*

Saint Teresa of Calcutta showed Mercy to the poorest of the poor in India. To her, every person she helped gave her another opportunity to show her love for Jesus. Teresa answered Christ's plea on the Cross: "I thirst," by showing Mercy to all of God's children, even the most forgotten.

 www.coronaerosarum.com

THE BOOK OF SEVENS

First Corporal Work of Mercy: FEED THE HUNGRY

God created man and woman as social beings. We are designed to live together in families, in communities, in larger groupings—tribes, clans, nations, peoples. God created us to be creatures who need to eat, drink, clothe our bodies, find shelter, and live together in harmony. One of the most basic human needs is a necessity we all share: food. We need to eat on a regular basis to sustain our strength, to remain healthy, and to flourish in all our endeavors.

In His Merciful Love, God gives His gifts freely—the sun, the rain, the seeds with which to grow fruits, vegetables, and grains. He fills the ocean with fish and sea creatures and the land with animals of all kinds. In God's ordered plan for creation there is enough food to sustain us all. But when that order is thwarted by the disordered failings of mankind—greed, hatred, cruelty, fear, selfishness—then those who have plenty do not share with those who are in want, and some people suffer and even die of hunger.

Every time we pray the Our Father—the prayer that Jesus taught us—we ask God to "give us this day our daily bread." This prayer asks God to sustain us in body and soul with what we need each day. One way God is able to provide for all of His children is when they share what they have. When we share what we have with those in need, we help to answer that prayer! We become God's hands, the instruments of His generosity. We give back to God a little of the

Queen Elizabeth of Hungary Feeds the Poor. Window at St. Bonaventure, Raeville. Photo Released to Public Domain by Ammodramus, 2010.

bounty with which He has blessed us; we show God the love He deserves to receive from us by showing Mercy to those in need.

We can make a real difference in feeding the hungry in three ways: 1. Supporting institutions that feed the hungry—Catholic Relief Services or other reputable groups that collect funds to feed the poor worldwide; 2. Working to make the world a better place by our support for more equitable laws, a kinder economy, and a more respectful and charitable society; 3. Giving our time and talents to local efforts to help with food drives, food banks, soup kitchens, and meals to shut-ins or neighbors who are in need.

Saint Teresa of Calcutta saw Jesus's face in every person she helped: "Whatsoever you do to the least of My brothers, that you do unto Me."

A Monk Sharing Food, Raccolta de' costume de Roma, 1819. ©Fae, 2014. CC BY-SA 4.0.

Second Corporal Work of Mercy
GIVE DRINK TO THE THIRSTY

Drinking water to relieve thirst is the most basic human need, even more immediate than the necessity for food. While it may be painful, a person can live for weeks without food. Without water, a person cannot live more than three to five days—in dry, hot conditions the time is measured in hours. Without water, organs begin to fail; a thirsty person goes into shock and dies.

While people in the poorest places may have water to drink, it may not be clean water. Many poor people suffer from diseases associated with unsanitary conditions—dysentery and parasites. A 2014 UNICEF Report found that 1,400 children *die every single*

Thirst, by William-Adolphe Bouguereau, 1886. Public Domain.

Rebecca at the Well, by Bartolomé Esteban Perez Murillo, before 1683. Public Domain.

day from these diseases. One out of every ten people in the world is forced to drink unsanitary water. A 2014 report by the World Health Organization estimates that universal access to clean water could save 2.5 million lives every year.

It is easy to feel helpless when reading statistics like these. What can one person do to change these crimes against humanity, which are also crimes against the ordered design of creation as God intended it? Supporting institutions that strive to alleviate suffering and disease can make a greater impact than one individual working alone. Working to build a more just world where the laws and economic policies share wealth and resources more equitably helps as well. Everyone may not be able to contribute in these ways, but everyone has the responsibility to pray for the success of these endeavors. Pope Saint John Paul II, in *The Christian Meaning of Human Suffering*, gave a deeper context to these issues and challenges us to find the power within ourselves to help:

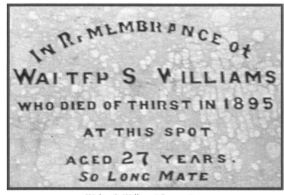

Walter S. Williams' Grave, 1895.
Photo ©SDowling CSIRO, 2003. CC BY-SA 3.0.

"We could say that suffering, which is present under so many different forms in our human world, is also present in order to unleash love in the human person . . . . The world of human suffering calls for, so to speak, another world: the world of human love; and in a certain sense owes to suffering that unselfish love which stirs in one's heart and actions. The person who is a 'neighbor' cannot indifferently pass by the suffering of another. . . ."

The Servant of God Father John Hardon wrote:

"When we ask for 'our daily bread,' we are asking for the God of Mercy to inspire countless Good Samaritans to reflect this mercy in their loving concern for the suffering of others."

Be a Good Samaritan!

Third Corporal Work of Mercy: CLOTHE THE NAKED

People who lack the necessities of life struggle to survive many different hardships. Some are poor, with no means of income. Some are sick and unable to provide for themselves and their families. Some are victimized by natural disasters—violent storms, floods, fires, droughts, or famine. Some are refugees fleeing from persecution and war, leaving behind all they owned to search for safety. These people need food and clothing to keep them healthy and give them hope for the future.

Clothing the naked means helping those who are unable to care for themselves. Donating

Evacuees from San Diego Wildfires Gather Clothes Donated by Area High Schools at Turner Field Naval Base. Public Domain.

clothing to charitable groups that distribute clothing to the needy is one way. Volunteering to assist local clothing drives is another way to lend a hand. You may be surprised by how much good you can do!

When Kellie Ross of Manassas, VA, discovered that some of the children in her son's class at school

American Red Cross WW1 Clothing Drive, c1917. National Archives. Public Domain.

could not walk properly because their shoes were too small, she decided to take matters into her own hands. In 2008, she founded *House of Mercy*, a free clothing store for the homeless and needy, where thousands of items are given to the poor each month. Many of the clothes are 'gently used,' but intimate attire and shoes are always new. Kellie felt strongly that the poor should always be treated with dignity; giving them new shoes and undergarments shows respect for their personal needs. Kellie summarized her experiences in this way: "I realized that our devotion to Divine Mercy is allowing God to use us as instruments to bring hope to the poor."

The love that we show when we share our bounty with the less fortunate should not become the selfish love of feeling good about ourselves. The charity of God is love that is not limited in any way but gives for the sake of giving. If we are to give back the love that God in His Mercy has shown to us, it should not be with any thought of recompense, either material or spiritual. We should leave it to God to decide the worth of our charity to others. Jesus promised:

"Give and it shall be given to you. A good measure, pressed down, shaken together, running over, will be put into your lap; for the measure you give will be the measure you get back."   *(Luke 8: 38)*

Fourth Corporal Work of Mercy:
SHELTER THE HOMELESS/WELCOME THE STRANGER

In the Middle Ages, faithful Christians went on **pilgrimage**—they traveled to faraway sacred places like the Holy Land, Rome, Compostello, Loretto, and other shrines devoted to saints and miraculous events. In those days, there were no motels! People carried a walking stick, a hat with a sea shell on it, and a drinking gourd—and they walked! Walking was a part of the pilgrimage—a penance, an effort to make amends for their sins, a way to open their hearts to the Will of God in their lives.

These pilgrims depended on the kindness of others to give them shelter along the way. It was customary hospitality for good Christians to shelter traveling pilgrims on their journey. While the situation is very different today, the spirit of welcoming those away from home can live on in the way we treat out-of-town folks. Giving a stranger directions is one way; being patient with the car whose driver is uncertain about the roads is another.

But there is much more to this work of Mercy than being polite to travelers. Many people find themselves without proper shelter for different reasons—financial difficulties, wars, loss of jobs, old age, persecutions, storms, fires, floods, abuse, famines, illness, or alienation from their families. In 2005, a United Nations report found that, worldwide, one hundred million people were

Saint Elizabeth of Hungary Gives Shelter to the Poor.
St.Bonaventure Church, Raeville. Released to Public Domain by Ammodramus, 2010.

homeless. In 2014, the U.S. Department of Housing and Urban Development counted 578,424 homeless people in America.

Many valiant individuals and groups work with the homeless to alleviate their problems. Often the solutions require specific skills to work with people who are suffering, frightened, or troubled. Until you learn these skills, it may be best to leave this work to those trained to assist. Homeless people still need your financial and spiritual support. Donating/serving meals at a homeless shelter, collecting necessities for the homeless, and raising money to support these efforts are all critical aspects. However, offering prayers and sacrifices for the needs of the homeless is something everyone can do!

Homeless WWII Refugees at Caen Cathedral, France, in 1944. Public Domain.

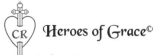
Fifth Corporal Work of Mercy: VISIT/COMFORT THE SICK

Attending to the physical needs of those who are infirm is basic to the Christian way. Natural law, the law written on our hearts, teaches us: "Do unto others as you would have them do unto you." When you are sick, injured, or in pain, you hope that someone will be there to take care of you, bind up your wounds, bring you food and medicines, help you heal, and keep you safe and warm. In these ways, all caregivers—doctors, nurses, medical staff, police, firemen, and rescue workers—practice this corporal work of Mercy.

The sick also need *comfort*; they need to know they are not alone and have not been forgotten. By taking time to visit them and bring them the comfort of your conversation and your prayers, you lift them up and lighten the burdens they carry. By sharing with them your faith and trust in God's Merciful Love, you can bring them spiritual healing. Each year four million people visit the Lourdes shrine where St. Bernadette prayed the rosary with the Blessed Mother. Mary showed her a special stream that was Our Lady's gift to the sick. Many visitors who come are seriously ill; they come to bathe in the waters of the miraculous stream, hoping for a physical cure. While there have been documented cures, not everyone is cured—but most go home healed in spirit.

Those who follow the Divine Mercy devotion say that the Divine Mercy Chaplet, when prayed while visiting the sick (even the comatose), is a powerful means of bringing grace and comfort to the sick and the dying. Saint Teresa of Calcutta lived a passionate ministry to the poorest of the poor—especially those who were left to die alone in the street. Teresa already belonged to an order of teaching sisters when she received a call from God to minister to the poorest of the poor. She left behind her comfortable convent to care for the forgotten. She began by giving comfort to an old man who was lying in a gutter dying. She

Visit the Sick. Released to Public Domain by Ammodramus, 2010.

vowed to bring comfort and dignity, even to just the last moments of these forgotten ones. In 1958, she opened her first "Home for the Dying" in Calcutta. She founded a order of sisters called the Missionaries of Charity. She opened orphanages, hospices, clinics, and leper houses, as well as new convents all over the world. By 2007, Missionaries of Charity operated 600 missions, schools, and shelters in 120 countries, run by 5,000 religious sisters and 450 religious brothers. A reporter stood amazed, watching as Mother Teresa bathed the leprous sores of a poor man. He exclaimed, "I wouldn't do that for a million dollars!" She replied, "I wouldn't, either! I do it for love of Jesus."

Mother Teresa's Home for the Dying. Released to Public Domain by Mark Makowiecki, 2005.

Sixth Corporal Work of Mercy
VISIT THE IMPRISONED/RANSOM THE CAPTIVE

In ancient times, it was sometimes possible to pay captors for the release of prisoners. Holding prisoners for ransom was common in the Middle Ages as well. While serving in a war between the warring city-states of Assisi and Perugia, a young Saint Francis was held for ransom for a year in a Perugian prison. From the time of the invasion of Spain in 711 by Moors from North Africa, the areas along the coast of Spain, France, and Portugal were made dangerous by warring factions, pirates, and privateers, who captured innocent bystanders and held them for ransom. Finding the means to free loved ones was a great financial challenge for families but was still considered an important work of Mercy.

St. John de Matha founded a Catholic order, called the Order of the Most Holy Trinity, to ransom Christians held captive by non-Christians. St. Peter Nolasco founded the Royal Order of Our Lady of Mercy, known as Mercedarians, who took four vows rather than the usual three [poverty, chastity, and obedience]; the fourth vow was *to take the place of a captive* in order to save the captive's soul. Our Lady of Mercy is also known as Our Lady of Ransom.

These days, it may not be possible to pay to free prisoners from jail, but it is still possible to help save their souls by showing them that they have not been forgotten. Life is prison is lonely and bleak, especially for those who have no one to visit them or write to them. Remembering them helps to show them that God loves them. God is Merciful and loves all His creatures with a love that is not based on our actions but upon His complete Generosity. All that God requires is that we ask for His Mercy.

Time in prison can be a time of penance for those who have committed crimes and caused others pain and suffering. Or time in prison can become a time of further deterioration, where the prisoner only grows in hatred and feelings of worthlessness. Whether prison time is a period of healing or relapse may depend upon showing the prisoner God's Mercy.

By practicing this work of Mercy—visiting

Abraham Ransoms His Brother Lot from Captivity, by Édouard Didron, 1881.

prisoners or supporting groups that minister to prisoners, we can make a real difference in the lives of those who have lost their way in life, helping them to return their hearts to the God who loves them.

Seventh Corporal Work of Mercy: BURY THE DEAD

The practice of praying for the dead goes back to the Old Testament. In the Second Book of Maccabees, the Jewish leader Judas returned to the battlefield after the Sabbath to bury the bodies of his soldiers who had died in a great battle two days earlier. As they began to collect the bodies, they found talismans honoring pagan gods that the slain men had been carrying "for good luck." This was a violation of the First Commandment—a terrible sin; everyone present felt that this sin was the cause of the death of these slain men, who were punished for their unfaithfulness to God. Judas took this occasion to invite all present to pray for the souls of the dead, that God might forget their sins and permit the dead to participate in the resurrection. Judas still hoped in the Mercy of God to free them from their sins after death:

"It is therefore a holy and wholesome thought to pray for the dead, that they may be loosed from their sins." (12: 46)

The early Christians endured many persecutions, and many were martyred because they would not worship the false gods of the Romans. They were executed in terrible ways for their faithfulness to the One True God. Because they died for the Faith, they are called **martyrs**. Their bodies were left unburied as an added disgrace. But other Christians came secretly to remove the martyrs' bodies and be properly buried. This was very dangerous, since they themselves would receive the same fate if they were caught. They took the martyrs' bodies to caves under Rome where they gave

A Procession in the Catacomb of Callistus, by Alberto Pisa, 1905. Public Domain.

the martyrs a proper funeral. The Christians would attend Holy Mass in the catacombs, gathering around the bones of the martyrs to pray with them. To this day, the altar in most Catholic churches contains a little reliquary that holds the bones of a saint.

The Bible tells us that on the last day, the Trumpet shall sound and the dead shall be raised. **This means that our bodies will be returned to us.** Those who have been faithful to God's laws and relied on His Mercy will go to Heaven, and those who have not will go to hell. Our bodies should be treated with respect even in death. For this reason, it is a Corporal Work of Mercy to treat *all* human remains with respect.

One way that we can show respect is by making sure that those who have died receive a proper burial. When we attend a funeral, we show the respect and compassion that is appropriate, no matter the circumstances. A soul that is precious to God has gone on to its eternal destiny and should be remembered with mercy. Our presence gives comfort to those who have lost a loved one. It is important to participate in prayer services for the dead and to always remember to pray for the Souls in Purgatory, in particular for those souls who have no one to pray for them.

Bury the Dead, by Édouard Didron, 1881. Saint-Front, France. Photo ©Père Igor, 2012. CC BY-SA 3.0.

The Seven Spiritual Works of Mercy

The Spiritual Works of Mercy go hand-in-hand with the Corporal Works of Mercy. Both these sets of Works help us to give and to receive the Merciful Love of God in this life. The Corporal Works relieve the needs of our bodies through the food, water, clothing, shelter, and medicine we need to care for our bodies. The Spiritual Works care for our hearts and souls by giving and receiving knowledge of the Love of God, correcting sinfulness, bearing wrongs, forgiving, consoling, and praying.

As important as food, water, and shelter are to our bodies, the Spiritual Works of Mercy are **even more important**! Our physical needs may be immediate and critical to health and happiness here on earth, but our need for the Spiritual Works of Mercy is even greater because they bring us guidance, peace, and comfort in this life—and lead us to the eternal joys of Heaven.

The Spiritual Works of Mercy go to the heart of the Christian message of sharing the Love of God with others. Caring for the physical needs of others through the Corporal Works of Mercy gives the Christian message of charity a concrete reality for those in need of food, clothing, water,

> ### Spiritual Works of Mercy
> 1. Instruct the Ignorant
> 2. Counsel the Doubtful
> 3. Admonish Sinners
> 4. Bear Wrongs Patiently
> 5. Forgive Offenses Willingly
> 6. Comfort the Afflicted
> 7. Pray for the Living & Dead

shelter, or medicine. But meeting the physical needs of those in want is only half the job.

Sharing the Spirit of the Living God with those who are suffering in mind and heart speaks to the deepest needs of the human family. It is a Mercy to offer others the knowledge of God in order to bring them into the Light of His Love. Counseling those who are confused and admonishing those who are trapped in the darkness of sin continues to lead them into the Light of God's Love.

Bearing with the wrongs that others do to us and forgiving them freely gives witness to the power of God's Love to forgive, to renew, to wipe away our trespasses, and to begin again to love and be loved as God made us to love each other. Never forget "Forgive us our trespasses as we forgive those who trespass against us" means that we are asking God to forgive us *in the same way that we forgive others*!

Consolation offered in times of distress or sadness and prayers that lift up the needs of our brothers and sisters (both in life and in eternity) can be a sweet source of peace that builds on the graces of the Holy Spirit, the Great Comforter.

www.coronaerosarum.com

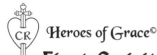

First Spiritual Work of Mercy: Instruct the Ignorant

The first Spiritual Work of Mercy is the most basic. Before anyone can love God or try to do His Will, they must learn about who God is and what He desires us to do to be pleasing to Him. It is an important work of Mercy to instruct those who have not heard the Good News of the Gospel and to give them the means to know God so that they can serve Him in this world and then be happy with Him in Heaven for all eternity.

What greater gift can a person give than the truth? Jesus explained it best: "You will know the truth and the truth will make you free" because "everyone who commits a sin is a slave to sin. . . . So if the Son makes you free, you will be free indeed" (*John 8: 32, 34, 36*). The freedom Jesus offers is not license to do whatever a person might want to do, but the ability through knowledge and grace to choose what will set you free from your own weaknesses and failings to become the person God truly made you to be.

At the Last Supper on Holy Thursday, Jesus prepared to offer Himself to God the Father as the Perfect Sacrifice to atone for all the sins and failings of mankind. He told His Apostles: "I Am the Way, the Truth, and the Life. No one comes to the Father except through Me" (*John 14: 6*). In this way, Jesus made it clear that a knowledge of His Person is the path to loving union with God—which is the greatest joy of Heaven. To know Jesus is to find the gate, the key, and the path to eternal peace, joy, and love.

The Catholic Church is distinguished by "*Four Marks*"—this means these four attrib-

Instruct the Ignorant. Released to Public Domain by Havang, 2012.

utes must all be present for the Church to remain the authentic Church established by Jesus Christ when He was here among us. We name these *Four Marks* every Sunday at Mass when we recite the Creed: "One, Holy, Catholic, and Apostolic." The last *Mark*, "Apostolic," refers to the fact that the truths of the Faith have been handed down from the Apostles to each generation—without ever being changed. The Church may alter its ceremonies, its laws, its customs, but never the truths the Apostles passed down.

Our generation is charged with the same duty and privilege that every generation before us for the past 2,000 years has fulfilled: to pass on the truths of the Faith to the next generation—without allowing these truths to be changed or corrupted. To instruct the ignorant is to share with others the rich treasures of the Faith that has been passed down to us.

The Great Commission

The last words Jesus spoke to His Apostles before He ascended into Heaven are called The Great Commission*:*
"All authority in Heaven and on earth has been given to Me. Go therefore and make disciples of all nations, baptizing them in the Name of the Father and of the Son and of the Holy Spirit, and teaching them to obey everything that I have commanded you. And remember, I am with you always, to the end of the age." (*Matthew 28: 17-20*)

Second Spiritual Work of Mercy: COUNSEL THE DOUBTFUL

St. Francis de Sales. ©Philippe Alès, 2012. CC BY-SA 3.0.

After a person has been given instruction in the truths of the Faith, the work of supporting that Faith continues throughout life. There are many reasons why people might doubt the Faith. Maybe they were not taught all the truths of the Faith so they understood them clearly. Maybe they experienced great suffering or some tragedy that led them to question God's love and mercy. Maybe their sense of the importance of following God's laws is lacking in some way—possibly because they are distracted by the cares of daily life, or troubled by temptations that pull them away from God, or indolent in the practice of their Faith. Whatever the cause, it is a great mercy to advise the doubtful to take heart and continue to follow the teachings of Christ and His Church on earth. Jesus promised us the Truth. He told us that He is the Way to God. He offers us a share in the very Life of God. It is our task to remind each other that Jesus is truly with us and leading us home to the Father.

A wonderful example of a saint who counseled the doubtful is Saint Francis de Sales. He lived in the early years of the Protestant Reformation, a time of great confusion about the truths of the Faith and the Church as handed down from the Apostles. As a young man, he attended a lecture on the heretical theory of "predestination" and concluded he was damned to hell. He became physically and spiritually sick until he prayed to the Blessed Mother for guidance and decided to dedicate his life to God.

De Sales became a priest and later a bishop, serving a diocese in Geneva, Switzerland, where most Catholics had fallen into the errors of Protestant Calvinism. He was undaunted in his efforts to reach out to these people through the written word in articles, broadsheets, and books and through his amazing gift for preaching. His diocese eventually became celebrated because the faithful became so well-instructed in the Faith!

Saint Francis de Sales' motto was: "He who preaches with love, preaches effectively." All his efforts to counsel those who were confused or doubted the Love of God and the teachings of the Church were performed with patience, charity, and respect. He understood that in giving counsel, it is important to show the gentleness that speaks more about the Love of God than words can express. As Saint Francis of Assisi once said, "Preach always—and, if necessary, use words."

It is part of human nature to wonder and to doubt, but God has promised us that keeping the Faith and doing His Will leads us to salvation.

The Mustard Seed

Jesus said, "Truly, I tell you, if you have faith the size of a mustard seed, you will say to this mountain, 'Move from here to there,' and it will move, and nothing will be impossible for you. (Matthew 17: 20)

www.coronaerosarum.com

Third Spiritual Work of Mercy: ADMONISH THE SINNER

St. John the Baptist, by Leonardo da Vinci, before 1519. Louvre, Paris. Public Domain.

and His Merciful Love. Through our faith, we know that the surest way to peace, joy, and love is to follow the Good Shepherd Jesus Christ. But Jesus calls us to do more than follow; He asks us to lead others to Him and to Heaven. For this reason, we need to try to inspire others to do the right thing according to God's Will and to seek His forgiveness when necessary.

Saint John the Baptist took great pains to admonish a very important sinner in his day: King Herod. Herod Antipas (the son of the Herod who murdered the Innocents) had taken his brother's wife Herodias and was living in the sin of adultery with her. Saint John was not intimidated by the fact that he was calling out the King in a public way. He confronted Herod and Herodias, telling them that "it is not lawful for you to have your brother's wife" (*Mark 6: 18*). John said it was his duty to admonish them. Otherwise, their sin would be on John's head, too, if he did not perform this work of Mercy to try to save them from their transgressions against God's laws.

John paid dearly for his admonishment. Herodias hated John the Baptist. Through trickery, she arranged to have John put to death. Herod did not want to execute him because he knew John was a "righteous and holy man" (*Mark 6: 20*). Though Herod did not want to give up his sinful ways, he knew that John was right.

Sometimes it is not wise or respectful to admonish the sinner on our own. At those times, it may be best to encourage a sinner to approach a priest for advice and for the grace of the Sacrament of Penance. The graces of the Sacrament not only heal the sinner's soul but also strengthen the sinner to avoid those temptations in the future.

Sometimes, it may be counterproductive to openly admonish a sinner—especially if our words might push them further away from God and His laws. In any case, it is always possible to admonish the sinner by giving good example through the way we live our own lives, the choices we make, and the way our humble words and actions reflect the Merciful Love of God.

Today we live in a diverse society where people make many different choices about how they choose to live. It can be very challenging to "admonish the sinner" using the moral standards of the Catholic Church. To some extent, it may not be fair to judge the actions of others by our yardstick of faith, but at the same time we should always remain open to the opportunity to share the wisdom of our Faith with those who are seeking God

Fourth Spiritual Work of Mercy: BEAR WRONGS PATIENTLY

Bear Wrongs Patiently. Released to Public Domain by Havang, 2012.

Human beings have an instinct for justice. Small children know when a toy belongs to them—if someone tries to take their toy, they yell, "Mine!" and try to grab it back.

We know when we are treated unfairly. Our first reaction is usually to try to set the matter straight. When others wrong us, we want our rights. People sometimes resort to anger, harsh words, or physical violence in an attempt to settle the matter. But Jesus calls us to love. Bearing Wrongs Patiently is the Spiritual Work of Mercy that calls us to respond to unkindness with kindness, to meet violence with peace, to face such cruelty and hatred with patience.

There are two excellent reasons why Jesus

calls us to respond with love when we are wronged by others. If we endure the cruelty of others with patience and mercy, it confounds those who wrong us and challenges them to rise above their own cruelty. As Saint Paul said:

> *"If your enemies are hungry, feed them; if they are thirsty, give them something to drink; for by doing this you will heap burning coals on their heads."* (Romans 12: 20)

By offering them love for hate, we show them there is another, better way. We set an example of love that reflects the Merciful Love of God— who loves all His children and wants to save us all.

Bearing Wrongs Patiently is the best way to respond to the offenses of others for another reason. Responding with patience helps us to rise above our desire to "get back at" an offender. If we respond to an offense with the same unkindness, it changes us. We become no better than those who try to hurt us. Holding onto offenses can even damage our health and take away our peace of soul.

Just as Jesus offered Himself on the Cross for all the sins and offenses of mankind, we can offer our sufferings, uniting them with Jesus's Sacrifice out of love for Him. This is called "redemptive suffering" because it brings comfort to Jesus and helps to heal the world of its offenses. Bring all your sufferings to Holy Mass and offer them to Jesus with a loving heart.

Fifth Spiritual Work of Mercy: FORGIVE OFFENSES FREELY

"Father, forgive them, for they know not what they do."

(Luke 23: 34, Douay-Rheims ed.)

The Crucifixion, by Henry Thomas Bosdet. Released to Public Domain by Man vyi, 2013.

When we are hurt by others, it is very difficult to forgive them, especially when the offense is not an accident or omission, but a deliberate act intended to offend or harm. Jesus came into the world to teach a better way—He came to perfect the Old Law of "an eye for an eye." Jesus calls us to repay evil with good:

"Do not resist an evildoer. But if anyone strikes you on the right cheek, turn the other also. . . . I say to you, Love your enemies and pray for those who persecute you, so that you may be children of your Father in Heaven; for He makes His sun rise on the evil and on the good . . . . Be perfect, therefore, as your Heavenly Father is perfect." (Matthew 5: 39, 44, 46)

Jesus did not just teach this truth with words—He set an example by His actions in the most dramatic way possible. As Jesus hung on the Cross, dying in an excruciatingly painful way for crimes for which He was completely innocent, He prayed for those who were persecuting, insulting, and torturing Him. He asked the Father to forgive them all and even argued their case by pointing to their ignorance of the full meaning of their actions.

Jesus set a powerful example for us to follow. Given the love and mercy God shows us for our own sins and imperfections, we must try to forgive each other freely and with love. If we cannot find the resolve to forgive for love of our enemies, we can forgive for love of Christ, who died to save each one of us from sin and death. *"If you do not forgive others, neither will your Father forgive you"* (Matthew 6: 15).

Sixth Spiritual Work of Mercy: COMFORT THE AFFLICTED

Jesus, the Good Shepherd, by Alfred Handel. St. John's, Ashfield, NSW, Australia. ©Toby Hudson, 2009. CCBY-SA 3.0.

The word "affliction" refers to the misery, distress, or grief that can be caused by sickness, loss, calamity, or persecution. Such suffering might be physical, mental, spiritual, or all three. The Spiritual Work of Mercy to "Console the Afflicted" calls us to minister to those in pain by giving them comfort, love, and support in their anguish. Our efforts should be to help them to heal in spirit and face their challenges with hope.

Even in our darkest hour, we must always remember that Jesus is our Good Shepherd. No matter what the challenges or afflictions, He brings us hope. He does not ask us to go where He has not already been. He knows all of our suffering: He took it all on Himself. Jesus has already fought the battle with suffering, sin, and death—and has won the final victory and opened the gates of Heaven for us. He leads us home to the Merciful Love of God.

As people of hope, we must bring hope and consolation to a world filled with affliction—to help others experience the healing Love of God.

Psalm 23

The Lord is my Shepherd, I shall not want.
He makes me lie down in green pastures;
He leads me beside still waters;
He restores my soul.
He leads me in right paths
for His Name's sake.
Even though I walk through
the darkest valley,
I fear no evil; for You are with me;
Your rod and your staff—they comfort me.
You prepare a table before me
In the presence of my enemies;
You anoint my head with oil;
My cup overflows.
Surely goodness and mercy shall follow me
All the days of my life,
And I shall dwell in the house of the Lord
My whole life long.

Seventh Spiritual Work of Mercy: PRAY FOR LIVING & DEAD

When we are baptized, we become the children of God. We become part of God's family. Another name for this family is the "Communion of Saints." The word "saints" here includes more than Saints in Heaven. In his Epistles, Saint Paul called all faithful Christians "the saints." So, in that sense, anyone who is baptized is a "saint." Thus, the Communion of Saints includes all the baptized on earth, in Heaven, and in Purgatory. If you are baptized, you are already a member of the Communion of Saints!

What keeps us together as a family is Jesus in the Blessed Sacrament. When we receive Jesus in the Holy Eucharist, we become members of His "Mystical Body." We are His arms and legs, His feet and His hands. We share in the graces that flow from the Sacraments. Because of this, we can share these graces with each other!

When we pray to God, we ask Him to help us in our needs, and He gives us what we need to be pleasing to Him. Not only that, we can ask our brothers and sisters in Heaven to pray for us before the Throne of God. They can ask God to share the graces and blessings they have received as Saints with us. We are a family, and we help each other to share the Merciful Love of God. We can even ask God to help our brothers and sisters in Purgatory. Our prayers may even lessen their purification, making it possible for them to enter Heaven more quickly!

We can also ask God to help others here and now with their needs. It is good to make a habit of praying for every member of your family every day. It is pleasing to God when we lift

Christ in Gethsemane, by Heinrich Hofmann, 1890. Riverside Church, NYC. Public Domain.

up their needs and desires as well as our own. We should even pray for our enemies, for those who hurt and persecute us. Jesus said,

> "I say to you, Love your enemies and pray for those who persecute you, so that you may be children of your Father in Heaven; for He makes His sun rise on the evil and on the good, and sends rain on the righteous and on the unrighteous." *(Matthew 5: 44-45)*

It is an act of love to pray for others, and an especially great act of Mercy to pray for those who offend us. God loves each of us—with all our sins and faults, He cares for us as His family.

Even though Jesus was the Son of God, Second Person of the Blessed Trinity, He spent many hours in prayer, asking His Father to give His Apostles and followers the graces to endure all the trials that lay before them. We should follow Jesus' example in prayer, asking God to grace us in life and death with His Merciful Love.

It is a holy and wholesome thought to pray for the dead.

(2 Maccabees 11: 46)

Seven
Catholic Devotions

For over twenty centuries since Christ walked among us, the Catholic Church has guarded the truths of the Faith that Jesus taught His Apostles. These truths are revealed to us in the Holy Bible and in <u>T</u>radition [*the oral teachings given us by the Apostles*]. These teachings are the foundation of what the Catholic Church professes and teaches.

As an artist celebrates the beauty of nature in a painting or a poet expresses deep feelings about an experience, people over the centuries with special respect for Jesus, Mary, or the Saints have celebrated their love with what we call **Devotions**. These expressions of love were sometimes inspired by personal spiritual experiences of the Love of God, the motherly care of Mary, or the kind intercession of the Saints. In some cases, the practice of these Devotions began as a result of personal communication with Jesus, Mary, or a Saint.

Catholics are required to believe all "public revelation," that is, the Bible and Tradition (including the Church's formal pronouncements on Articles of Faith). Public revelation ended with when Saint John the Evangelist died.

We are not required to believe any revelations that were received privately since the death of St. John. However, the Catholic Devotions in this book have been approved by the Church—because these Devotions *do not disagree with public revelation.* The faithful who embrace these Devotions are encouraged (not required) to do so. Always make sure to check with the Church before believing in any private revelations.

The Devotions in this book open our hearts to celebrating the beauties of our Faith. These Devotions provide us with added ways to show our love for Jesus, Mary, and the Saints. These Devotions help us appreciate the Truths that Jesus has revealed to us and continues to reveal to us—just as a beautiful flower opens to the sun.

The practice of these Devotions is like an embrace of love between Heaven and earth. When we practice these Devotions, Heaven graces us with new lights about what our Faith means, as well as with an abiding sense of peace that comes from nurturing a real and personal relationship with God, His Mother, the Angels, and the Saints.

The Sacred Heart of Jesus

Solemnity: Nineteen Days after Pentecost

In the Bible, the word "heart" refers to the center of a person's soul. The Old Testament often refers to the Heart of God to describe God's Merciful Love for us, as in Hosea: "I was to them like those who lift infants to their cheeks" (11: 4). Jesus loves us with the Divine Heart of the Living God and the compassionate human Heart of our Savior, who surrendered to the Cross for us and whose human Heart was wounded by the lance on Good Friday.

Sacred Heart. ©Reinhardhauke,2010. CC BY-SA 3.0. commons.wikimedia.org/wiki/File:Lodève_Saint-Fulcran_cathedral_stained_glass_window378.JPG

Many medieval mystics were devoted to the Heart of Christ. Then, in 1673, a French nun named Margaret Mary Alacoque received a vision of Jesus. He stood before her as she prayed in the chapel before the Blessed Sacrament. His Heart was visible and glowed with light. He spoke to her, naming Twelve Promises to those who show devotion to His Sacred Heart. He asked that the faithful make reparation for the sufferings of His Heart—by receiving Holy Communion more frequently, by making a weekly Holy Hour, and by going to Mass on nine consecutive First Fridays. Jesus asked that His Sacred Heart be honored with its own Feast Day. Approved for the whole church in 1856, the Feast of the Sacred Heart is celebrated on the nineteenth day after Pentecost, always on a Friday.

Jesus revealed His Heart to show us how deeply He loves each one of us and to help us understand how much He suffered because He loves us— both by His Passion and Death and by the ingratitude of those who do not return His Love. He asks us to adore His Heart, to love Him in return for His Love, to consecrate an image of the Sacred Heart in a place of honor, and to make reparation for those who have not yet turned to His Heart.

"Behold this Heart that has so loved men . . . instead of gratitude I receive from the greater part [of mankind] only ingratitude."

THE TWELVE PROMISES OF THE SACRED HEART

1. I will give them all the graces necessary for their state in life.
2. I will give them peace in their families.
3. I will console them in all their troubles.
4. I will be their refuge in life and especially in death.
5. I will abundantly bless all their undertakings.
6. Sinners shall find in My Heart the source and infinite ocean of mercy.
7. Tepid souls shall become fervent.
8. Fervent souls shall rise speedily to great perfection.
9. I will bless those places wherein the image of My Sacred Heart shall be exposed and venerated.
10. I will give priests the power to touch the most hardened hearts.
11. Persons who propagate this devotion shall have their names eternally written in my Heart.
12. In the excess of the mercy of My Heart, I promise you that my all-powerful love will grant to all those who will receive Communion on the First Fridays, for nine consecutive months, the grace of final repentance: they will not die in my displeasure, nor without receiving the Sacraments; and My Heart will be their secure Refuge in that last hour.

The Sacred Heart.©Andreas F. Borchert,2009. CC BY-SA 3.0. commons.wikimedia.org/wiki/File:Glengarriff_Church_of_the_Sacred_Heart_Left_East_Window_Sacred_Heart_2009_09_08.jpg

Devotion to the Blessed Sacrament

The Miracle of Lanciano

Angels Adore Jesus in the Blessed Sacrament. ©Jacek Jalicki, 2014. CC BY-SA 3.0.
commons.wikimedia.org/wiki/File:2014_Nysa,_Bazylika_św._Jakuba_i_św._Agnieszki,_witraż.jpg

Devotion to the Blessed Sacrament has existed since the time of the Apostles. Many early martyrs died because they protected the Blessed Sacrament with their lives. Jesus in the Blessed Sacrament should always be treated with the greatest reverence and respect. The gift of Jesus's Presence among us brings us into a close personal relationship with God, who loves us more than we can ever imagine.

Over 1,000 years ago, extraordinary miracles happened with the Blessed Sacrament, such as the Miracle of Lanciano. Popes decided to foster greater devotion to Jesus in the Blessed Sacrament. One way to show devotion is to attend a Holy Hour with Benediction. During Holy Hour, a consecrated Host is taken from the Tabernacle and placed in a golden vessel called a Monstrance so that Jesus in the Blessed Sacrament is visible for adoration. Prayers may be said or participants may adore in silence.

At the end of Holy Hour, the priest covers his hands with a veil and raises the Monstrance. He makes the Sign of the Cross with the Monstrance. This is called Benediction. All those present here receive a blessing from Jesus Christ Himself!

Benediction with Monstrance. Released to Public Domain by The Photographer, 2013.

In Lanciano, Italy, in the 8th century, a priest prepared to say Mass—but he doubted the miracle of Jesus's Body and Blood. He said a prayer asking God to help him believe.

Then, when he said the words, "This is My Body," the Host in his hands turned from bread into Human Flesh and began to bleed on the altar cloth. The wine turned into Blood in the chalice. The people in the church also saw this.

The Host and the Blood were placed in a reliquary to honor Jesus for the gift of this special miracle. The Pictures at right show this reliquary, the Blood, and the Host. These Holy Relics from that Mass are 1,300 years old.

In 1971, a professor of anatomy and pathology named Odoardo Linoli was allowed to examine these Elements. His study found that the Blood contains the normal proteins found in *living* blood—with no added preservatives. The blood type is the same as the Blood found on the Shroud of Turin. <u>The Host is a slice from a Human Heart.</u>

> **Most Holy Trinity, I adore You! My God, my God, I love You in the Most Blessed Sacrament.**

Top Image:
Lanciano Reliquary.
Released to Public Domain
by Junior, 2006.

Middle Image:
Detail of Reliquary
showing Sacred Blood of
Lanciano Miracle. ©AFC
Photo, 2014. commons.
wikimedia.org/wiki/File:
2_miracolo.jpg

Bottom Image:
Detail of Reliquary
showing Sacred Host.
©AFC Photo, 2014.
commons.
wikimedia.org/wiki/
File:3_miracolo.jpg

The Divine Mercy

Feast Day: **The Sunday after Easter**

Helena Kowalska was born in 1905 in Poland. Her parents were peasants who struggled after World War I to make a living, but her family had deep faith in God. At the age of seven, as she gazed at Jesus in the Blessed Sacrament, she decided to consecrate her life completely to God. After attending school for three years, she asked permission to join a convent, but her parents refused. When she was 16, they sent her to work as a maid to help support them. At 19, she had a vision in which Christ told her to join a convent. She left that night without telling her parents, taking a train to Warsaw. After being turned away by every convent because she lacked a dowry, the Mother Superior of the Sisters of Our Lady of Mercy struck a bargain with her—if she could work long enough to pay for her habit, they would allow her to

Saint Faustina. Public Domain.
Marians of the Immaculate Conception, 2009.

join. Faustina worked for a year as a maid to raise the funds. In 1926, she received her habit and took the name Maria Faustina of the Blessed Sacrament. She served in several convents as gardener, cook, or porter, assigned to the humblest jobs due to her poor education. After contracting tuberculosis, she went to a farm to recuperate. Returning to her convent, she received a vision on February 22, 1931; Jesus appeared to her dressed in a white robe, with rays of red and white light emanating from His Sacred Heart. He told her to "paint an image according to the pattern you see, with the signature, 'Jesus, I trust in You'." Her spiritual director Father Sopocko found an artist named Eugene Kazimirowski, who followed Faustina's instructions as he painted the image to the left. Jesus asked for a Feast of Divine Mercy on the Sunday after Easter, saying that, on that day, the Ocean of His Mercy would grant complete forgiveness to souls who approach Him: **"Mankind will not have peace until it turns with trust to My Mercy."**

Faustina also revealed that Jesus gave the Chaplet of Divine Mercy as a prayer to be said for three reasons: "to obtain mercy, to trust in Christ's Mercy, and to show mercy to others." The formula is simple—prayed on a rosary, it is a popular prayer at the hour of death, to obtain mercy for the dying person's soul. Go the TheDivineMercy.org for specific instructions on how to pray this powerful devotion for God's saving Mercy.

At the request of her director, Sister Faustina kept a diary entitled *Divine Mercy* describing her visions and conversations with Jesus. In the mid 1930s, Faustina's health deteriorated again, just as Divine Mercy pamphlets and holy cards were first made public by Father Sopocko. Faustina died October 5, 1938, at the age of 33. Pope Saint John Paul II canonized her in 2000, declaring the universal Feast of Divine Mercy the same day.

Jesus, I Trust in You

Divine Mercy by Eugeniusz Kazimirowski, 1939. Public Domain.

The Holy Name of Jesus

Feat Day: **January 3**

The Name of Jesus as written in Hebrew: It is pronounced "Ye-shu-a"

When the Angel Gabriel came to Mary to announce that God had chosen her to be the Mother of the Savior, the Angel told her the Name that God had chosen for her Son:

> Behold, you will conceive in your womb and bear a Son, and you shall call His Name Jesus. *(Luke 1: 31)*

When an Angel came to Joseph in a dream, the Angel explained that Mary's child would be conceived by the Holy Spirit, adding:

> She will bear a Son, and you shall call His Name Jesus, for He will save His people from their sins.
> *(Matthew 1: 21)*

It is significant that Jesus' Name was given directly by God the Father. In Jewish custom, it was the father's prerogative to name his child, and so God shows in this way that He is the Father of Jesus. In Hebrew, the name Jesus means "God saves"—indicating that Jesus was being born to fulfill God's promise to Adam and Eve that He would send a Savior into the world to save mankind from sin and death and thus open the Gates of Heaven.

Many passages in the Bible refer to the importance of the Name of Jesus and the power that is contained in His Name. Saint Paul defines the nature of this commanding power as above all other names:

> God has highly exalted Him and bestowed on Him a Name which is above every name, so that at the Name of Jesus, every knee should bow, in Heaven and on earth and under the earth, and every tongue should confess that Jesus Christ is Lord, to the glory of God the Father.
> *(Philippians 2: 9-11)*

The Dream of King Philip II, by El Greco, 1580. Public Domain.

Just before His Passion and Death, Jesus Himself told the Apostles about the power of His Name:

> Truly, truly, I say to you, if you ask anything of the Father, He will give it to you in My Name. *(John 16: 23)*

In the beginning of the *Acts of the Apostles*, after Jesus had ascended into Heaven, the Apostles began to preach the Good News; Peter invited others to believe with these words:

> Repent, and be baptized every one of you, in the Name of Jesus Christ for the forgiveness of your sins; and you shall receive the gift of the Holy Spirit.
> *(Acts 2: 38)*

After that, Peter passed a crippled man sitting by the temple gate begging for money. Peter took pity on him and said, "I have no silver and gold, but I give you what I have; in the Name of Jesus Christ of Nazareth, walk." The man was miraculously cured and got up and walked, but the Pharisees were angry. They asked Peter: "By what power or by what name did you do this?" Peter replied:

> There is salvation in no one else [but Jesus], for there is no other Name under Heaven given among men by which we must be saved. *(Acts 4: 12)*

The Church has encouraged prayer in the Name of Jesus as a great source of healing and spiritual power. The letters IHS were used by early Greek Christians to symbolize the Name of Jesus; IHS are the first three letters of the Greek spelling of Jesus: IHSOUS. The Romans used also this symbol: in Latin IHS stands for Iesus Hominem Salvator, translated "Jesus, Savior of Mankind."

Released to Public Domain by Moransky, 2008.

THE BOOK OF SEVENS

The Holy Face of Jesus

Feast Day: **Shrove Tuesday** [*the day before Ash Wednesday*]

Sister Marie of St. Peter. PD.

In 1843, Jesus appeared to Sister Marie of St. Peter, a French Carmelite nun. During this vision, Sister Marie saw Saint Veronica wipe the Face of Jesus on the way to Calvary; Jesus then asked Sister Marie to begin a Devotion to His Holy Face in reparation for His sufferings on Good Friday, as well as the ongoing blasphemies and sacrileges against His Holy Name and against the Holy Eucharist—which Jesus described as like "poisoned arrows." He dictated *The Golden Arrow* prayer to her to make reparation for these offenses—offenses that continue to wound Him to this day.

Venerable Leo Dupont, a French lawyer nicknamed *The Holy Man of Tours*, was famous for his good works and for re-inspiring the French people to the Catholic Faith after the French Revolution. He heard about Sister Marie's visions and began promoting Devotion to the Holy Face. Thirty years later, this devotion was approved by Pope Leo XIII in 1885.

Ven. Leo Dupont. PD.

Saint Thérèse of Lisieux had a deep devotion to the Holy Face—she chose to be called "Thérèse of the Child Jesus and of the Holy Face." Her poems about the Holy Face of Jesus still inspire many to practice this Devotion today.

In 1936, Blessed Maria Pierina, an Argentinian nun, received a vision from Jesus in which He told her: "I desire that My Face, which reflects the intimate pains of My Spirit, the suffering and the love of My Heart, be more honored. He who meditates upon Me, consoles Me."

In other visions of Jesus and Mary, Blessed Maria was instructed to create a medal with an image based upon the Face of Jesus on the Shroud of Turin, the burial cloth in which the Body of Jesus was wrapped after His death and which today still bears a miraculous Image of His crucified form [*see photo negative of the Holy Face from the Shroud at wikipedia.org/wiki/Secondo_Pia*]. Then, in 1958, Pope Pius XII approved this Devotion, as well as the Holy Face Medal based on the Shroud Image. He declared the Tuesday before Ash Wednesday to be the Feast of the Holy Face of Jesus. The painting at right is based on the artist Domenico Fetti's study of the Face on the Shroud of Turin. The picture at left is believed to be the Face of Jesus as preserved on Veronica's Veil.

Devotion to the Holy Face of Jesus is a beautiful way to express our love and gratitude to Jesus for His Passion and our deep reverence for Him in the Holy Eucharist, as well as a meaningful way to experience the season of Lent.

The Face of Christ on the Mannopello Cloth.
Public Domain.

Saint Thérèse of Lisieux. PD.

Bl. M. Pierina. PD.

THE GOLDEN ARROW PRAYER

May the Most Holy, Most Sacred, Most Adorable, Most Incomprehensible and Ineffable Name of God be always praised, blessed, loved, adored, and glorified in Heaven, on earth, and under the earth, by all the creatures of God, and by the Sacred Heart of Our Lord Jesus Christ, in the Most Holy Sacrament of the Altar. Amen.

—As dictated by Jesus to Sister Marie of Saint Peter

"The Veil of Veronica," by Domenico Fetti, 1622.
National Gallery of Art, Washington, DC. Public Domain.

PRAYER TO THE HOLY FACE

O Holy Face of my sweet Jesus, by that tenderness of love and unspeakable grief with which the Blessed Virgin Mary beheld Thee in Thy painful Passion, grant that our souls may share in that great love and great sorrow, and fulfill more perfectly the Holy Will of God. Amen.

—as dictated by Jesus to Blessed Maria Pierina Di Micheli

The Holy Rosary & the Battle of Lepanto

Feast Day: *October 7*

Painting of the Battle of Lepanto, by an anonymous artist, late 16th century. National Maritime Museum, London. Public Domain.

The Battle of Lepanto has been called one of the most decisive battles in history. Because Turkish forces threatened the eastern edge of Europe and the future of Christianity itself, the Pope made a desperate plea to the nations of Europe to raise armies. He also called on every Christian to pray the Rosary for victory, begging the Blessed Mother to protect Christianity from being conquered by the Moslems. On the day of battle, October 7, 1571, the forces of Don Juan of Austria, with other European armies, defended the Christian world against Turkish invasion, defeating them in the naval battle at Lepanto. Because of this amazing victory over superior forces, the Pope declared October 7 to be the **Feast of the Holy Rosary**. Eventually, the Church declared the month of October the **Month of the Holy Rosary**.

The Rosary is an amazing prayer with a long, fascinating history. The word "rosary" comes from the Latin **rosarium**, meaning "rose garden." Seen this way, each prayer said in the Rosary is a rose in Mary's crown. Mary herself is known by the title "Mystical Rose," and her heart has been compared to a "secret garden" in which God takes delight. The Immaculate Heart is always depicted with a crown of roses around it; Mary is often pictured being crowned with roses by the Holy Trinity.

The order of prayers in the Rosary came about in this way: in ancient times, priests, monks, and nuns daily chanted in Latin the **Divine Office**, which over the course of a month includes all 150 Psalms in the Book of Psalms in the Bible. But lay people could not read or speak Latin, so it was decided that saying 150 Hail Marys could substitute among lay people for praying the Office. The most popular form of the Rosary that we use today came from Saint Dominic, who had a great devotion to Mary.

The Rosary is a powerful prayer on many levels. The vocal prayers are repeated in a way that calms the persons praying and helps focus their thoughts on spiritual things. The Rosary has five decades; each decade consists of one Our Father, ten Hail Marys, and one Glory Be. Each decade has a "Mystery" attached to it—a prescribed theme upon which to meditate while praying. There are four sets of Mysteries—Joyful, Sorrowful, Luminous, and Glorious; each set of Mysteries has five themes that match up with its five decades (*see chart below*). When we meditate on these Mysteries, we ponder special events in the life of Jesus through the eyes of His Mother Mary. In this way, Mary shows us the joys, teachings, sorrows, and glories of her Son's life, leading us to her Son—and, thus, to our own salvation. By meditating on the life of Christ through her eyes, we become like Mary—we become secret gardens in which God delights. Then we, too, can go out into the world, bringing others to Christ, just as Mary always leads us to her Son Jesus.

Mysteries	First Mystery	Second Mystery	Third Mystery	Fourth Mystery	Fifth Mystery	Which Day to Say Mysteries
Joyful	The Annunciation	The Visitation	The Nativity	The Presentation of Baby Jesus in the Temple	The Finding of the Child Jesus in the Temple	**Mondays, Saturdays, & Sundays in Christmas Season**
Luminous	Jesus' Baptism	The Wedding Feast at Cana	The Proclamation of the Kingdom	The Transfiguration	The Institution of the Holy Eucharist	**Thursdays**
Sorrowful	Jesus' Agony in the Garden	Jesus Is Scourged at the Pillar	Jesus Is Crowned with Thorns	Jesus Carries His Cross	Jesus Is Nailed to the Cross & Dies	**Tuesdays, Fridays, & Sundays in Lent**
Glorious	The Resurrection	The Ascension	The Descent of the Holy Spirit	The Assumption of the Blessed Mother	The Coronation of the Blessed Mother	**Wednesdays & most Sundays**

Our Lady of Sorrows

Feast Day: **September 15**

On the Feast of Our Lady of Sorrows, the Church meditates on the many sorrows that the Blessed Mother had to endure as the Mother of Christ. While her role in salvation history is a glorious one, it was not without intense sadness. Seeing the sufferings Christ endured through the eyes of His pure mother helps us to bring their impact into sharper focus.

Traditionally, Devotion to the Sorrows of the Blessed Mother, also called *Mater Dolorosa* [*Sorrowful Mother*], focuses on seven events in Christ's life with painful impact on His Mother:

1. Simeon's Prophecy/Christ's Circumcision
2. The Flight into Egypt
3. The Loss of the Child Jesus for Three Days
4. Meeting Jesus on the Way of the Cross
5. Standing at the Foot of the Cross for the Three Hours of Jesus' Agony on the Cross
6. Receiving Jesus' Body from the Cross, *or* The Piercing of Christ's Side with a Lance
7. Placing Christ's Body in the Tomb.

In religious art, the Sorrowful Mother is often depicted with her heart pierced by seven swords and crowned with flames. The seven swords correspond to the seven sorrows. The swords are derived from Simeon's Prophecy to Mary at Jesus' Presentation in the Temple: *"A sword will pierce through your own soul also"* (Luke 2: 35).

The flames burning up from her heart signify the Love of God that always burned in her heart. Mary never desired anything that was not the Will of God. It is fitting and valuable to meditate upon her sufferings because she always gave her will to God—even as she stood at the Foot of the Cross and watched her beloved Son endure His final agony. Mary knew that God had willed Christ's Sacrifice to save souls. Mary offered her dying Son to God knowing that this was the price that must be paid to save mankind from sin and death. In this way, Mary is truly our Mother in Heaven because she loves us with a complete, selfless, mother's love. She gave all she treasured most for each one of us: her pure and holy Son, the Son of God, Jesus Christ.

Several Devotions are associated with the *Mater Dolorosa*, the most famous being the *Sorrowful Mysteries of the Rosary*. As we pray each decade of the Rosary, we meditate on Christ's sufferings as seen through His Mother's eyes: His Agony in

Our Lady of Sorrows, Santa Maria del Alcor, Seville. Released to Public Domain by Ajjb, 2007.

the Garden, Scourging at the Pillar, Crowning of Thorns, Carrying the Cross, and Death on the Cross.

Another popular Devotion to the Sorrowful Mother is the *Chaplet of the Seven Sorrows* (or *Dolors*). This chaplet has seven groups of seven beads. Praying a *Hail Mary* on each bead, we meditate on each of the Seven Sorrows using each of the seven groups of beads. This Chaplet can be prayed all at once, or spread over the entire week by praying one set of seven Hail Marys a day while meditating on each of the Seven Sorrows on successive days. For instance, on Sunday you could pray seven Hail Marys for the First Sorrow, Simeon's Prophecy. On Monday, you could pray seven Hail Marys and meditate on the Flight into Egypt. When you meditate, try to imagine yourself as Mary and how you might feel. Think about how Mary experienced the life of Christ as an eyewitness of love.

In 1983, a visionary named Marie-Claire Mukangango in Rwanda received a vision of Mary (approved by the Church) in which Mary told her:

> *"Recite the Rosary every day, and also the Rosary of the Seven Sorrows of Mary, to obtain the favor of repentance."*

Seven Catholic Prayers

THE SIGN OF THE CROSS

In the Name of the Father, and of the Son, and of the Holy Spirit. Amen.

1.   OUR FATHER

Our Father, who art in Heaven,
hallowed be Thy Name.
Thy Kingdom come, Thy Will be done,
on earth as it is in Heaven.
Give us this day our daily bread,
and forgive us our trespasses,
as we forgive those who trespass against us.
And lead us not into temptation,
but deliver us from evil. Amen.

2. HAIL MARY

Hail Mary, full of grace, the Lord is with thee.
Blessed art thou amongst women,
and Blessed is the Fruit of thy womb, Jesus.
Holy Mary, Mother of God,
pray for us sinners, now
and at the hour of our death. Amen.

3. GLORY BE

Glory be to the Father, and to the Son,
and to the Holy Spirit:
as it was in the beginning, is now, and
ever shall be, world without end. Amen.

4. THE MORNING OFFERING

O Jesus, through the Immaculate Heart of
Mary, I offer Thee all my prayers, works, joys,
and sufferings of this day in union with all the
Masses said throughout the world today, for
the intentions of the Sacred Heart, for the
reunion of all Christian Churches, for world
peace, in reparation for outrages against the
Sacred Heart of Jesus and Immaculate Heart
of Mary, and for the intentions of the Holy
Father and all apostles of prayer. Amen.

5. ACT OF CONTRITION

O my God, I am heartily sorry for having
offended You, and I detest all my sins, because
of Your just punishments, but, most of all,
because they offend You, my God, who are
All-Good and worthy of all my love. I firmly
resolve, with the help of Your grace, to
confess my sins, to do penance, and to amend
my life. Amen.

6. PRAYER TO SAINT MICHAEL

St. Michael the Archangel, defend us in battle.
Be our protection against the wickedness and
snares of the devil. May God rebuke him, we
humbly pray. And do thou, O Prince of the
Heavenly host, by the Power of God, cast into
hell Satan and all the evil spirits who prowl
about the world seeking the ruin of souls. Amen.

7. THE MEMORARE

Remember, O most gracious Virgin Mary, that
never was it known that anyone who fled to
thy protection, implored thy help, or sought
thine intercession, was left unaided. Inspired
by this confidence, I fly unto thee, O Virgin of
virgins, my Mother. To thee do I come, before
thee I stand, sinful and sorrowful. O Mother of
the Word Incarnate, despise not my petitions,
but in thy mercy hear and answer me. Amen.

PRAYER TO THE HOLY SPIRIT

Come, Holy Spirit,
fill the hearts of Thy faithful
and enkindle in them the Fire of Thy Love.
Send forth Thy Spirit and they shall be created,
and Thou shalt renew the face of the earth!

THE BOOK OF SEVENS

 *Heroes of Grace©*

Appendix of Important Catholic Lists

The Four Marks of the True Church
1. **ONE**: United in belief, rituals, prayers
2. **HOLY**: Directed to achieving holiness
3. **CATHOLIC**: Universal, welcoming all
4. **APOSTOLIC**: Protects & preserves the authentic teachings of the Apostles

The Twelve Apostles
1. Peter [formerly named Simon]
2. Andrew
3. James the Greater/Compostella [son of Zebedee]
4. John [son of Zebedee]
5. Philip
6. Matthew
7. Thomas
8. Jude Thaddeus
9. Bartholomew [also called Nathaniel]
10. James the Lesser [son of Alphaeus]
11. Simon [the Zealot]
12. Judas Iscariot [later replaced by Matthias]

The Four Gospels/Evangelists [Symbol]
1. Matthew [Angel or Human Face]
2. Mark [Lion]
3. Luke [Winged Ox]
4. John [Eagle]

The Five Books of the Pentateuch [the Torah]
1. Genesis
2. Exodus
3. Leviticus
4. Numbers
5. Deuteronomy

The Ten Commandments
1. I am the Lord thy God. Thou shalt not have strange gods before Me.
2. Thou shalt not take the Name of the Lord thy God in vain.
3. Remember to keep holy the Lord's day.
4. Honor thy father and thy mother.
5. Thou shalt not kill.
6. Thou shalt not commit adultery.
7. Thou shalt not steal.
8. Thou shalt not bear false witness against thy neighbor.
9. Thou shalt not covet thy neighbor's wife.
10. Thou shalt not covet thy neighbor's goods.

The Two Great Commandments
1. You shall love the Lord your God with all your heart, with all your soul, and with all your mind.
2. You shall love your neighbor as yourself.

The Eight Beatitudes *(Matthew 5: 1-11)*
1. Blessed are the poor in spirit, for theirs is the Kingdom of Heaven.
2. Blessed are those who mourn, for they shall be comforted.
3. Blessed are the meek, for they will inherit the earth.
4. Blessed are those who hunger and thirst for righteousness, for they shall be filled.
5. Blessed are the merciful, for they will receive mercy.
6. Blessed are the pure in heart, for they will see God.
7. Blessed are the peacemakers, for they will be called children of God.
8. Blessed are those persecuted for righteousness' sake, for theirs is the Kingdom of Heaven.
9. Blessed are you when people revile you and persecute you and utter all kinds of evil against you falsely on My account. Rejoice and be glad, for your reward in Heaven is great!

The Seven Precepts of the Church
1. Keep Sundays and Holy Days of Obligation holy by attending Mass and resting from servile work;
2. Keep the days of fasting and abstinence that are appointed by the Church;
3. Go to Confession at least once a year;
4. Receive Holy Communion at least once a year during the Easter season;
5. Support our parishes and priests;
6. Not marry within a certain degree of kindred;
7. Join in the missionary apostolate of the Church.
—Prescribed for the USA by the 3rd Plenary Council of Baltimore in 1886

Holy Days of Obligation in the USA
1. Feast of the Immaculate Conception of Mary, **December 8** *(December 9 if December 8 is on a Sunday)*
2. Christmas Day, **December 25**
3. Solemnity of Mary, **January 1***
4. Ascension Thursday (moved to the following Sunday in some dioceses)
5. Assumption of the Blessed Mother, **August 15***
6. All Saints Day, **November 1***

* If any of the feasts with an asterisk falls on a Saturday or a Monday, the obligation to attend Holy Mass is "abrogated"—meaning that the obligation is suspended for that particular calendar year only. The others are never abrogated.